"Help Me, I'm Sad"

"Help Me, I'm Sad"

Recognizing, Treating, and
Preventing Childhood
and Adolescent Depression

DAVID G. FASSLER, M.D.
AND LYNNE S. DUMAS

VIKING

VIKING
Published by the Penguin Group
Penguin Putnam Inc., 375 Hudson Street,
New York, New York 10014, U.S.A.
Penguin Books Ltd, 27 Wrights Lane,
London W8 5TZ, England
Penguin Books Australia Ltd, Ringwood,
Victoria, Australia
Penguin Books Canada Ltd, 10 Alcorn Avenue,
Toronto, Ontario, Canada M4V 3B2
Penguin Books (N.Z.) Ltd, 182–190 Wairau Road,
Auckland 10, New Zealand

Penguin Books Ltd, Registered Offices:
Harmondsworth, Middlesex, England

First published in 1997 by Viking Penguin,
a member of Penguin Putnam Inc.

10 9 8 7 6 5 4 3 2 1

AUTHOR'S NOTE
The individual experiences described in this book
are based on actual clinical work with children and their families.
In all cases, however, specific details and identifying information
have been modified to protect the privacy of the patients.

The ideas, procedures, and suggestions contained in this book
are not intended as a substitute for consulting with your physician.
The reader should regularly consult a physician in matters relating
to health and particularly with respect to any symptoms that
may require diagnosis or medical attention.

Grateful acknowledgment is made for permission
to reprint the "Coddington Life Events Record" from
"The Significance of Life Events as Contributing Factors in
the Diseases of Children" by J. S. Heisel, S. Ream, R. Raitz,
M. Rappaport, and R. D. Coddington, *Journal of Pediatrics*, 1973,
vol. 83. By permission of Mosby–Year Book, Inc., St. Louis, Missouri.

LIBRARY OF CONGRESS CATALOGING IN PUBLICATION DATA
Fassler, David, M.D.
"Help me, I'm sad" : recognizing, treating, and preventing childhood and
adolescent depression / David G. Fassler, M.D., and Lynne S. Dumas.
      p.   cm.
   Includes bibliographical references and index.
   ISBN 0-670-86547-8
   1. Depression in children—Popular works.   I. Dumas, Lynne S.
II. Title.
RJ506.D4F37   1997
618.92'8527—dc21   97-4235

This book is printed on acid-free paper.
(∞)

Printed in the United States of America
Set in New Aster
Designed by Virginia Norey

Acknowledgments

The support, encouragement, and assistance of many people have made this book possible. From an early age, my parents, Joan and Leonard, taught me how to listen and showed me the power of words and ideas. My sister, Ellen, has been a constant source of inspiration, practical advice, and honest feedback.

I would also like to acknowledge the following friends and professional colleagues who generously shared their clinical insight and experience: Leslie Conroy, M.D.; Bill Rae, Ph.D.; Bob Keane, L.I.C.S.W.; Nancy Cotton, Ph.D.; Melinda Macht Greenberg, Ph.D.; Liz Brenner, L.I.C.S.W.; and Kathy Gutting, M.S.W.

I want to thank my colleagues at Choate: Stu Koman, Ph.D.; Gail Hanson Mayer, R.N.C.S., M.P.H.; Maggie Moran, R.N., M.H.S.A.; Ken Minkoff, M.D.; Larry Cohen, C.P.A.; Chris Paterson, Ph.D.; and Nina Rosenberg, M.M.H.S., and the staff of the Anna Jaques Child Psychiatry Program at the Amesbury Health Center for their ongoing contributions to this project.

I am also grateful to my collaborator, Lynne Dumas, who kept me on track with a combination of patience, persistence, flexibility, and humor which allowed us to be productive and to have fun at the same time.

Further, both Lynne and I want to thank our agent, Loretta Barrett, and, of course, our insightful and responsive editor, Mindy Werner. We also appreciate the administrative contributions of Pat Cahill, Sue Niquette, Laurie Crawford, Kathy Talbert, and Tracey Allen. And our thanks go to Elise Marton, for her valuable editorial insights and guidance.

Many of the ideas in this book evolved through the influence of numerous professional mentors—both clinical and administrative—who encouraged me to ask questions and allowed me the flexibility to find my own answers. These include Al Solnit, M.D.; Sam Rofman, M.D.; Morris Wessel, M.D.; Mel Lewis, M.D.; Donald Cohen, M.D.; Bill Ayres, M.D.; Don Gair, M.D.; Paul Cotton, M.D.; Bruce Gibbard, M.D.; Helen Beiser, M.D.; Myron Belfer, M.D.; Ron Geraty, M.D.; Jennifer Stolz, Ph.D.; Bob Pierattini, M.D.; Kyle Pruett, M.D.; Jim Comer, M.D.; John Schowalter, M.D.; Larry Stone, M.D.; David Pruitt, M.D.; Shelly Weiner, M.D.; Bob Lenox, M.D.; and Douglas Betts, M.D.

Throughout my professional career, I have also received tremendous support from the American Academy of Child and Adolescent Psychiatry. I am particularly thankful to Mary Crosby and Virginia Anthony for their ongoing assistance and friendship, and for encouraging me to pursue my interest in childhood depression. Additionally, I appreciate the support we have received from the American Psychiatric Association, the American Medical Association, the National Alliance for the Mentally Ill and its affiliate chapters—with special thanks to Carolyn Sanger and Ben Coplan—and the Journey of Hope, particularly Joyce Burland, Ph.D.

Last, I am grateful to my child patients and their families—my true teachers—and to the many other children and adults who generously contributed their stories, impressions, and experiences to this book.

—D.G.F.

Contents

Introduction

The first time I saw Dana, she was a charming seven-year-old with short brown hair and enormous blue eyes. Her parents had brought her to see me at the urging of Dana's teacher, who was concerned about changes she'd noticed in the little girl's behavior. Dana had always been a quiet, cooperative child, but recently she'd gotten into several fights with her fellow first graders, pinching and biting them at the slightest provocation. She'd even given one young classmate a black eye.

Dana's parents, too, had noticed a change in their daughter's behavior. Over the last few months, she had become very sad and withdrawn, refusing to play with the other children in the neighborhood. She was reluctant to tell her parents what was bothering her and rebuffed their efforts to cheer her up.

Dana and I spent our first session just getting to know each other; after she explored the games I keep in my office, we played a round of checkers, then read a book she picked from the collection on my shelves. The second time we met, however, I asked her to draw me a picture of a person. She complied, drawing a simple stick figure of a girl with two eyes, long hair, and a big frown. "Can you tell me what she's doing?" I asked.

"She's crying," Dana answered. Then she added tears to the figure's face and printed the words "I'm sad" in uneven letters next to it.

"How come the girl in the picture is so sad?"

"Because she has no friends."

"What does it feel like to be sad?"

"Like I'm sadder than anyone in the whole world. I stay in my room and cry. Sometimes I get so sad I want to run away."

We talked a little more and then, later in the session, I asked her if she had ever thought of hurting herself.

"One time I was so sad I wished I would go to sleep and not wake up," Dana said softly, staring down at the drawing in front of her. Then, as tears welled up in her eyes, she picked up a crayon and added two words to the top of her picture: "Help me."

It's hard to imagine—and heartbreaking to realize—that a child as young as Dana could feel so hopeless, helpless, and depressed. Yet as she and I worked together, it became clear that her emotions went beyond the normal sadness that all kids feel from time to time. Dana's emotions were more intense, overwhelming, and enduring, interfering with her ability to play with her friends, or to continue her daily activities at home and at school. Her energy level had dropped, she'd lost weight, and her sleep was often disrupted by bad dreams. I also spoke with Dana's pediatrician, and together we determined that she was in good health—that is, she had no physical problems that would explain her symptoms. This information, combined with the fact that Dana's symptoms had continued over several months, led me to conclude that the youngster was clinically depressed.

Up until the late seventies, few people, including most mental health professionals, would have agreed. No one thought that children could suffer from real depression; there wasn't even an official diagnosis for childhood depression until 1980. Sure, clinicians believed, kids got sad once in a while, but they grew out of it. Young children just weren't emotionally mature enough to get depressed.

Today, however, we know that children can and do become clinically depressed. Such depression is not just a phase or an unhappy stage of normal development; it's a real and identifiable illness—even in children as young as Dana.

What could cause such young children to become clinically depressed? Genetics, biochemistry, early experiences, and a variety of other factors, all of which I detail in the pages that follow. But right up front, let me say this: Depression is *not* caused by poor parenting—so don't blame yourself. If your child develops depression, it isn't because you weren't a good enough mom or dad.

That is not to say that the way you parent your children has no effect on their emotional health. Clearly, for example, a youngster who has been abused is much more vulnerable to depression than a child who has not suffered so.

We also know that once a youngster becomes depressed, parents can play an important role in helping that child overcome his illness. Alert moms and dads can identify the earliest signs and symptoms of depression in their youngster, get him the professional help he needs, and work closely with the child's therapist to support early and appropriate treatment.

And fortunately, treatment for childhood depression is highly effective. Individual therapy, family therapy, medication, and work with a child's school can all help a youngster successfully overcome depression. Through my work as a child and adolescent psychiatrist, I have learned that children respond best to a comprehensive plan of treatment which often includes a combination of these approaches.

But here's what I find most hopeful and exhilarating: I believe that *childhood depression is preventable*, if not in all, then at least in many cases. And the key to prevention lies in you, the parent. By *parenting for resiliency*, which means raising your children in a way that develops their emotional adaptability, you can help your youngsters learn how to overcome life's challenges—from moving to a new neighborhood to changing schools to coping with loss—without becoming clinically depressed. By parenting for resiliency, you can reduce your children's risk for depression by raising their natural resistance to this illness, which will help them not only now but well into adulthood. What's more, since research has already taught us that "early onset depression" is "highly predictive of adult problems"—which simply means that depressed kids are more likely to become depressed grown-ups—it is very likely that early, effective treatment of depressed children will be able to help prevent depression in adults as well.

I am not alone in my convictions. The National Mental Health Association is so sure that childhood depression is preventable that in 1994 it issued recommendations encouraging depression-prevention programs in all fifty states. A report entitled *Reducing Risks for Mental Disorders*, prepared by the Institute of Medicine that same year, also stressed the importance of prevention. In it, Robert J. Haggerty, M.D., the chair of the Institute's Committee on Prevention of Mental Illness, says that proper, proactive parenting often can stop such mental illnesses as depression before they occur "much as immunization prevents infectious diseases." Marie Kovacs, Ph.D., a psychologist at Western Psychiatric Institute and Clinic in Pittsburgh and a leading researcher in the field of childhood depression, echoes that belief when she says, "If you want to make a real difference in depression, you have to do something before the kids get sick in the first place. The real solution is psychological inoculation."

All this encouraging news has led me to write this book, the title of which was inspired by Dana, my young patient. In it, I offer practical, understandable information that will help you distinguish normal, healthy sadness from the debilitating illness that is clinical depression. You'll learn the symptoms of clinical depression and the best ways to ensure that your depressed child gets the help he or she deserves. Finally, and just as important, you'll learn what you can do to prevent childhood depression in the first place, so that you can help your youngster enjoy a happy, healthy childhood and adolescence and grow into a confident, well-adjusted, and emotionally secure adult.

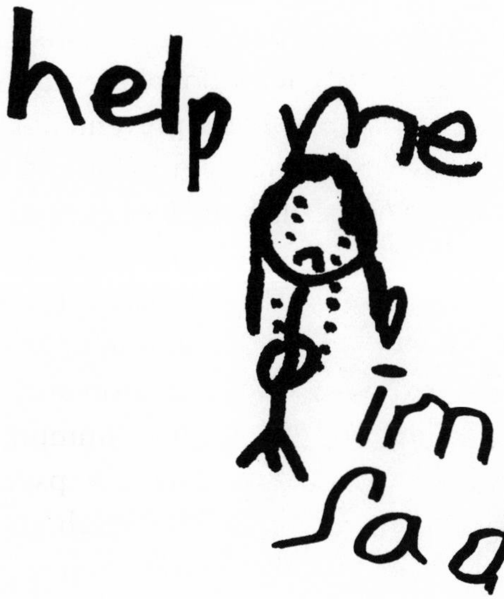
help me
im
sad

Chapter

1

When Sad's Good,
When Sad's Bad

Four-year-old Caroline was playing alone in the doll corner at her preschool. She was arranging the dolls in their house and holding a quiet conversation with them. Her teacher watched from a short distance and thought, "What a beautiful child, but so solemn and reserved." By the time she was three, Caroline had taught herself to read; in her former day-care center, she tended to shy away from other children and spent much of her time curled up alone with her favorite books.

When Caroline entered primary school, she'd become even more of a "loner." The teacher's comments on her straight-A report cards usually described her as a "serious child" with a "quick mind" who "seems to have trouble making friends." Still, it came as a shock to everyone when, at age eight, Caroline took a detour home from school one day and, without a word to anyone, slowly but determinedly walked into the middle of a busy four-lane highway.

"What do you think you're doing?" the policewoman who rescued Caroline asked. At first the youngster was silent, her eyes downcast. Then, in a soft, emotionless voice Caroline responded: "I wanted a car to hit me. I wanted to die. I don't want to be alone anymore."

■ ■ ■

Every parent wants to raise a healthy child who will become a happy, self-confident adult. It is the ultimate aim and best reward of child rearing. But that very desire makes it difficult for even the most well intentioned parents to acknowledge that their child seems too sad, too often.

Of course, all children feel unhappy from time to time. Sadness is a normal, natural response to many life events, from losing a soccer match or failing a test to moving away from old friends or losing a loved one. But when that sadness runs too deep, lasts too long, or occurs too often, it may be a sign of clinical depression, even in very young children like Caroline.

For many years, childhood depression went unrecognized. Many mental health professionals believed children weren't emotionally mature enough to experience true depression. As mentioned, it wasn't until the early 1980s that clinicians and researchers began to realize that childhood depression was a distinct, recognizable disorder.

So we now know that childhood depression exists. And the number of depressed kids is disturbing. The National Institute of Mental Health estimates that as many as 2.5 percent of all American youngsters under the age of eighteen—or over 1.5 million children and adolescents—are seriously depressed. The American Academy of Child and Adolescent Psychiatry places the number of "significantly" depressed children and adolescents even higher, at 5 percent, or 3.4 million youngsters. But since childhood depression is frequently overlooked, misunderstood, and misdiagnosed, I would not be surprised if we soon learn that the figure is much higher. In fact, after reviewing the research conducted with children and teenagers, I believe that *over one in four youngsters will experience a serious episode of depression by the time they reach their eighteenth birthday.*

Equally upsetting is the strong link between major depression and suicide, particularly in young people. On average, one young person (under age twenty-four) kills himself every two hours in this country, according to the American Association of Suicidality (AAS). And many more young people try. AAS reports that there are 100 to 200 attempts for every completed suicide among youths fifteen to twenty-four; other estimates run as high as 300 attempts. Even among children age twelve and younger, experts estimate that at least one in 100 has attempted suicide.

Studies show that some 60 percent of all high-school students have had thoughts about taking their own life, and that at least 9 percent have actually attempted suicide at least once. The rate of suicide among teens has more than doubled over the past thirty years, making suicide the second leading cause of death among children ages fifteen to nineteen!

Of course, not every child who attempts suicide is depressed. Some kids make an attempt while under the influence of drugs or alcohol. While not technically attempting suicide, others put their lives in jeopardy on a "dare" from friends. However, the majority of children who try to kill themselves are seriously depressed.

More Depression—or More Diagnoses?

There still isn't enough substantive research on childhood depression, and almost none that looks at the same children over long periods of time. But studies do suggest two significant trends:

- First, more and more children are crossing the line between normal sadness and clinical depression;
- Second, these children are becoming clinically depressed at earlier and earlier ages.

These statements raise important questions: Is childhood depression truly on the rise? Or are doctors simply recognizing the problem more often?

While no one knows for sure, I offer a qualified yes to both questions. Child psychiatrists like myself, as well as other mental health care professionals, have become more skilled at spotting depression in very young children, so we may well be diagnosing it more often. We are also realizing that many children previously diagnosed with other mental health problems, such as attention deficit hyperactivity disorder or conduct disorder (in which children become argumentative or unmotivated) are actually suffering from an *underlying* depression.

We are also learning that childhood depression often *coexists* with other emotional and behavioral problems. A child may suffer from an anxiety disorder *and* have many signs and symptoms of clinical depression, creating a diagnostic dilemma for clinicians. This situation can also complicate treatment: Since there's a tendency to focus on only one aspect of a child's problem, the doctor, parent, and child are often left wondering why, after treatment for that problem, the youngster is still having difficulties. It may well be, then, that the increased number of children now diagnosed with clinical depression in part represents a correction for the misdiagnoses—and incomplete diagnoses—of the past.

Here's another point: The psychiatric profession now knows that many depressed adults were depressed as kids, even though their problem may have gone unrecognized. This insight has led us to look more closely for signs of depression in young children so that their problems can be identified and treated early—which may be another reason why the number of reported cases of depression seems to be on the rise.

Clearly, then, we are identifying childhood depression sooner and more often than ever before. But both research and my own firsthand observations also lead me to believe that more children are actually experiencing symptoms that suggest clinical depression. This is one of the main reasons I decided to write this book. I want to help parents become more aware of the signs and symptoms of childhood depression so that they can spot trouble in their children as early as possible, and get them the help they so desperately need.

Normal Sadness vs. Clinical Depression

I don't want to frighten moms, dads, or caregivers, or in any way to suggest that feeling sad is bad, or that it *necessarily* signals clinical depression in a child. Even though we use the terms *sadness* and *depression* almost interchangeably in everyday conversation, they are really two distinct concepts. Sadness is a normal, healthy emotion; depression is a disease. The challenge lies in understanding and recognizing the difference. And that's not always easy, as the story of nine-year-old Michael reveals.

Michael was always on the go. He played baseball, soccer, and basketball, had lots of friends, and loved to go hiking and camping with his mom, dad, and eleven-year-old sister. But just before Michael was to start third grade, his father got an unexpected job promotion and moved the family to another state. Then, two days after they arrived in their new home, Michael's sister left for summer camp.

Suddenly, Michael's mother told me, he "became a different kid." He moped around the house all day and refused to play outside or ride bikes with his dad, something he used to love. He also seemed much more sensitive than usual, and was moved to tears at the slightest disappointment or frustration. After several weeks of this unusual behavior, Michael's worried mom brought him to see me.

Indeed, Michael seemed very sad. He was reluctant to talk or to make eye contact; instead, he just stared down at his shoes. I began talking with him and explaining what I knew about him and his family, eventually asking him to tell me about his old neighborhood. Gradually, he began to open up. He talked about his old school, how much he missed his friends and his sister, and how he thought it was a "totally dumb idea to move."

After we talked, I concluded that while Michael was very sad, he was not depressed. His sadness was a normal, healthy, and, I suspected, temporary response to some big changes in his life. I suggested that his parents be patient with him and give Michael more time to adjust to his new home and neighborhood. I offered to see the family again if Michael's symptoms seemed worse, but I suspected that he would start to feel better soon. In any case, I encouraged them to contact me again once school began.

When we spoke again in the early fall, Michael's parents reported that things were going much better. Once his sister had returned from camp and he had made a few friends in the new neighborhood, Michael had cheered up considerably. Although all summer long he remained extremely anxious about attending a different school, he liked his new teacher and his classmates. Michael, his mother concluded, was "back to normal again."

Loss, grief, disappointment, frustration, and change can lead to periods of significant sadness like the kind Michael experienced. But sadness is time limited; it doesn't go on uninterrupted for long intervals. For most children, sad feelings pass within hours or days, although, if the disruptions are as sudden and severe as they were for Michael, the distress can last longer.

Depression, on the other hand, is a cluster of signs and symptoms, including sadness, that are *intense, pervasive, and sustained* over a period of time. Depressive feelings tend to recur periodically and to disrupt the way a child functions from day to day. Had Michael been clinically depressed, his upset would probably have continued despite his sister's return. He might have had trouble making new friends and more difficulty settling in at school. He might also have continued to brood about his situation, having thoughts like "We moved because my parents don't really care about me" or "I'll never fit in here, and I'll never have any friends again." But in fact, although Michael was feeling very "sad" he was not truly "depressed." The former describes a normal, transient mood; the latter, a significant emotional disorder.

Here's another example that may help show the differences between sadness and clinical depression. Tracey, a fifteen-year-old, freckle-faced redhead, had been seeing her first real boyfriend for about six months. When he told her that he wanted to break up, Tracey was heartbroken. For a whole week, she came home from school and stayed in her room behind a closed door. When she reluctantly emerged for dinner, her eyes were red from crying.

A few days later, Tracey, normally a good student, failed a history test, explaining "I just couldn't study." Although her friends and family tried to cheer her up, she remained "in a funk." One night, she told her mother, "Guys are jerks!"

By the second week, however, her parents noticed that while Tracey was still subdued, she was crying less and decided to go out with a group of friends on the weekend. Within a few weeks of the breakup things were mostly back to normal, although she still felt sad occasionally, especially when something reminded her of her old boyfriend or the things they used to do together. By the next semester, Tracey had a new boyfriend.

Tracey's behavior was a typical, perfectly normal response to a fairly common adolescent event. She clearly felt hurt, sad, and confused. But these negative feelings, while powerful, were too short-lived to be considered true symptoms of depression. If she had felt hopeless and worthless for an extended period of time, if she had continued to fail tests and her grades began to drop, if she had refused to go to school or to spend time with friends, and/or if she had started to feel so bad about herself that she neglected her appearance and health, then Tracey may well have crossed the line to clinical depression. Once again, a child is clinically depressed when her negative feelings are so intense, pervasive, and sustained that they disrupt her daily routines and activities over a prolonged period of time.

Defining Clinical Depression

You can find a more precise definition of depression in *The Diagnostic and Statistical Manual of Mental Disorders* (*DSM*), the book that helps clinicians—and insurance companies—formally identify and diagnose emotional disorders. It's updated every few years or so, and the most recent edition—known in the field as the *DSM-IV*—offers specific criteria for the diagnosis of depression (see table on following pages). The *DSM-IV* classifies depression as a "mood disorder." It states that an individual has suffered a "major depressive episode" if certain symptoms persist for at least two weeks, including a loss of enjoyment in previously pleasurable activities, a sad or irritable mood, a significant change in weight or appetite, problems sleeping or concentrating, and feelings of worthlessness.

While I respect and often rely on the *DSM-IV* criteria, I also have some problems with them, especially when it comes to children. These criteria were developed from research with depressed adults. Although there are similarities between adult and childhood depression, there are also major differences, only some of which are addressed in the *DSM-IV*.

For example, the *DSM-IV* says that in order to be clinically depressed, an individual must have five or more symptoms that persist for two weeks. But depressed children often don't experience their symptoms for two weeks straight. Instead, they come and go frequently over a period of time.

Take thirteen-year-old Nathan. A bright child, he was very sensitive

---

Diagnostic Criteria for a Major Depressive Episode

A. Five (or more) of the following symptoms have been present during the same two-week period and represent a change from previous functioning; at least one of the symptoms is either (1) depressed mood or (2) loss of interest or pleasure.

1. Depressed mood most of the day, nearly every day, as indicated by either subjective reports (e.g., feels sad or empty) or observation made by others (e.g., appears tearful). Note: In children and adolescents, can be irritable mood.

2. Markedly diminished interest or pleasure in all, or almost all, activities most of the day, nearly every day (as indicated by either subjective account or observation made by others).

3. Significant weight loss when not dieting or weight gain (e.g., a change of more than 5 percent of body weight within a month), or decrease or increase in appetite nearly every day. Note: In children, consider failure to make expected weight gains.

4. Insomia [sleeplessness] or hypersomnia [getting too much sleep] nearly every day.

5. Psychomotor agitation or retardation [slow physical movement] nearly every day (observable by others, not merely subjective feelings of restlessness or being slowed down).

6. Fatigue or loss of energy nearly every day.

7. Feelings of worthlessness or excessive or inappropriate guilt (which may be delusional) nearly every day (not merely self-reproach or guilt about not being sick).

to disappointment or failure at school. He got extremely anxious before taking any test, and if he didn't get a perfect score, he became terribly sad for two or three days. By the next weekend, he would have snapped out of his "mood," which led his parents to believe that their son was simply a sensitive child, and that his behavior was nothing to be concerned about. But Nathan's emotional pattern—anxiety,

8. Diminished ability to think or concentrate, or indecisiveness, nearly every day (either by subjective account or as observed by others).
9. Recurrent thoughts of death (not just fear of dying), recurrent suicidal ideation [thoughts] without a specific plan, or a suicidal attempt or a specific plan for committing suicide.

B. The symptoms do not meet criteria for mixed episode [of depression and mania].

C. The symptoms cause clinically significant distress or impairment in social, occupational, or other important areas of functioning.

D. The symptoms are not due to the direct physiological effects of a substance (e.g. a drug of abuse, a medication) or a general medical condition (like hypothyroidism [underactive thyroid]).

E. The symptoms are not better accounted for by bereavement, i.e., after the loss of a loved one, the symptoms persist for longer than two months or are characterized by marked functional impairment, morbid preoccupation with worthlessness, suicidal ideation, psychotic symptoms, or psychomotor retardation.

(Reprinted with permission from the *Diagnostic and Statistical Manual of Mental Disorders*, fourth edition. Copyright 1994, American Psychiatric Association.)

followed by upset, and extreme sadness—occurred repeatedly, about once every two or three weeks. That made me suspect that he was not just sensitive, but depressed, even though no individual bout of sadness had ever lasted more than two or three days in a row.

I also think that the *DSM-IV* criteria, which are designed for mental health professionals, are too technical to be very helpful to parents, teachers, and caregivers. So instead of having the parents and caregivers I work with wade through the jargon of the *DSM-IV*, I encourage them to concentrate on one key question when trying to figure out whether their child is truly depressed: *To what extent do your child's sad feelings and behavior interfere with his everyday life and normal development?*

A little later on, when we discuss the signs and symptoms of depression, I'll help you arrive at a useful answer to this question. But right now, let's take some time to probe a little deeper into childhood depression and find out why so many kids develop this problem.

Why Kids Get Depressed

The study of childhood depression is complex. But there is one simple fact: Some children become clinically depressed while others do not. What causes depression in these children? While no one knows for sure, several theories exist. They focus on biological, psychological, behavioral, and family-related causes.

▪ Biological Theories

More and more mental health professionals have come to believe that biochemical makeup plays a key role in causing depression. Research shows that changes in the levels of certain chemicals in the brain can lead to the problem. Specifically, sufficient levels of three neurotransmitters, or chemical messengers in the brain—serotonin, which helps regulate sleep and memory; norepinephrine, which affects alertness and energy levels; and dopamine, which helps control emotion and movement—must be available between nerve cells to transmit the brain impulses that affect our emotions and moods. Reduced availability of these neurotransmitters can either bring on clinical depression or make a child more vulnerable to it when faced with life's many stressors.

Increasingly, researchers are coming to believe that certain people are born with the kind of brain chemistry that makes them depression prone. They also believe that some people may start out healthy but then experience a traumatic event—like the early death of a parent or abuse by a trusted caregiver—that actually changes their brain chemistry and makes them more vulnerable to depression.

Researchers observing depressed adults have noticed other biological differences, including changes in the behavior of their pituitary and adrenal glands, the glands that secrete hormones that affect the body's growth and its ability to respond to stress. As of yet, though, attempts to use these differences to help identify depression in children haven't proved useful.

We do know, however, that depression-like symptoms can be triggered by certain medications prescribed for children, including anticonvulsants (used to treat seizures), theophylline-related drugs (used for asthma), and steroids (used for chronic inflammations). Additionally, certain medical conditions, including thyroid problems, hypoglycemia (low blood sugar), anemia, mononucleosis, influenza, hepatitis, and diabetes may produce symptoms that look like those of clinical depression. But by using careful assessment techniques—which we'll discuss more fully in chapter 7—doctors are usually able to tell the difference between depression look-alikes and the real thing.

■ **Psychological Theories**

Much has been written about the psychological causes of depression in adults. And although a good deal of this literature links depression in adults to events that occurred in their childhood—the bitter divorce of one's parents, for instance—surprisingly little research has been done on the psychological causes of depression in children themselves.

But maybe that's not so surprising. After all, until relatively recently most mental health professionals didn't believe that children could develop depression. Now that most experts agree that childhood depression exists, however, they are beginning to apply psychological theories of adult depression to children. Many such theories abound, but here are a few that I think make particular sense.

The first has its roots in psychoanalytic theory. Based on the work of Sigmund Freud, it revolves around the idea that the loss of a "love object"—such as a parent, pet, or important relationship—can cause depression.

Traditional psychoanalysts also offer a second theory: that depression is really anger turned inward against the self. This means that a young child may be enraged at his dad for physically abusing his mom, but instead of confronting him—which is too scary and potentially dangerous—the child turns his rage on himself and becomes sad and eventually depressed.

Another theory: Depression is caused by an inability to attain a goal that the child views as important to his self-image. So, for example, a child who believes that he is a talented athlete may become depressed when he doesn't make the team. A youngster who sees herself as a very smart student may get depressed when she gets a B instead of an A. This is one of the reasons why setting unrealistic goals for children makes them more vulnerable to depression.

Finally, depression may center on a child's inability to separate from his parents. It is important and healthy for very young children to become attached to what we call their "primary caregiver," usually Mom or Dad. A strong, loving bond between you and your child creates the foundation for positive relationships throughout your youngster's life. But gradually, a healthy child develops enough self-confidence to become an independent, self-sufficient individual. When this does not occur—when the child remains so insecure that he feels he couldn't manage or even survive without his parents—he is vulnerable to depression.

▪ Behavioral Theories

We know that behaviors that are rewarded, or positively reinforced, tend to increase. If you enthusiastically praise your five-year-old each time he remembers to brush his teeth before bedtime, chances are he'll brush his teeth more often.

We also know that behaviors that are punished, or negatively reinforced, tend to disappear. If the rule is "no ball playing in the house," and you take away your child's TV privileges each time he disobeys that rule, eventually the indoor ball-playing will stop. (At least, that's the theory!)

But children can get depressed if they receive too much negative—and not enough positive—reinforcement. Suppose your mischievous child is always being punished at home; then she goes to school and, not being a very good student, gets lots of negative reinforcement there—she fails several tests, and to her teacher's obvious dismay, never seems to know the answer when called upon in class. In time, the overabundance of negative reinforcement can damage her sense of self-esteem, and increase her vulnerability to depression.

Another behavioral theory is that a child can actually "learn" to be depressed by observing behavior or events around him. For instance, if every time that you're faced with a stressful event—being turned down for a promotion, for instance—you go into a deep funk and refuse to get out of bed, you're teaching your child to respond to stress in a negative, unproductive way.

■ **Cognitive Theory**

Cognitive theory holds that negative-thinking patterns—poor perceptions of your self, your future, and the world around you—can lead to depression. A child who believes that she is worthless, that her future is bleak, and that the world around her is scary or unsafe, often becomes depressed—at least according to cognitive theory.

Then there's the concept of "learned helplessness." This idea suggests that when children are constantly told that they cannot control current or future events no matter what they do, they come to believe that they are helpless. Suppose, for instance, your daughter is having trouble in math. If you tell her that "girls are always bad in math," she'll start to believe that there's no point in trying to raise her grades. She thinks, "If girls are never good in math, and I'm a girl, nothing I do will help me improve. So what's the point of studying?"

According to cognitive theorists, this feeling of helplessness, of not being able to take control and improve negative aspects of life, can lead to depression.

A psychologist at Vanderbilt University, Judy Garber, Ph.D., has conducted a series of interesting studies based on the cognitive theory of depression. Her work shows that certain patterns of thought may predispose a child to react to life's stressful events by becoming depressed. In one study, for instance, Garber and her associates looked at fifth and sixth graders who got poor marks on their report cards. They found that those children who tended to be pessimistic, negative thinkers—that is, who blamed their bad grades on something in themselves that they could not change—tended to become depressed. Kids who felt that they could do something to improve their grades were sad for a little while but rebounded fairly quickly.

Interestingly, though—and this is something we will discuss in much greater detail later on in this book—Garber and other researchers have found that strong self-esteem can temper the effects of life's stressful events, even in pessimistic children with negative-thinking habits. If you can help your children feel good about themselves, you'll be creating a buffer that can help shield them from depression or, at the very least, greatly lower their risk.

■ Family Dynamics Theory

Many family therapists believe that childhood depression is caused by a dynamic, or pattern of relationships, that exists in the family. Sometimes, for instance, a child becomes depressed in order to stop her parents from arguing all the time. Without realizing it, the child may try to get her parents to pay more attention to her in order to divert them from their own problems.

Another possibility is that the child expresses depression *for* her parent. Let me explain. In my practice, many children have been referred to me with symptoms consistent with depression; for example, they are withdrawn and no longer want to participate in activities they once enjoyed. But once I meet their parents, it becomes quite clear that one or both of *them* is actually depressed. Although totally unaware of it, the child actually expresses depressive symptoms on behalf of her parent. How do we know? Because once the depressed parent (or parents) gets into treatment, the child's symptoms quickly disappear!

Children can also get depressed when there are conflicting expectations or relationships within their family. A typical example is a child who gets caught between his parents' differing value systems: One parent wants the child to go to public school, while the other insists on a private education. Or Dad wants his son to play football, while Mom is determined that he study the violin. No matter what the child does, he believes he will lose the favor of the parent who wanted him to do something else, so the youngster gets depressed.

Additionally, when parents are highly critical of their children— so much so that their kids feel they can never do anything right— youngsters often become depressed. Further, when children grow up in families where feelings are not openly expressed, and where keeping "family secrets" is the rule, depression may result.

I believe that each of these theories has merit, and that the cause of depression is probably a different combination of these factors for each individual child. But I also believe that even a child who is biologically, behaviorally, or cognitively predisposed to depression— or who lives in a dysfunctional family system—won't *necessarily* get depressed. In large part, that will depend upon a wide range of risk factors, such as temperament, relationships with loved ones, how the youngster is parented, and various life experiences, all of which increase or decrease the likelihood of depression. Let's explore them now.

Chapter

2

Is Your Child at Risk?

Some kids feel like killing their mom and dad and running away. Sometimes, I do too, like when they yell and scream. I think about running away, but mostly I just feel real bad, like I'm sick all the time. Sometimes, I want to hide.

—Randy, age ten

Despite the prevailing mythology, childhood isn't a time of uninterrupted joy. And it's perfectly normal for children to feel sad sometimes. But some kids become so unhappy—and stay that way for so long—that they are considered clinically depressed.

In chapter 1, we discussed how to tell the difference between sadness and depression, and the reasons why some children become depressed. But causes only explain the problem *retrospectively*, that is, *after the depression has appeared*. We also need to take a look at risk factors, which give us information *prospectively*, that is, *before depression occurs*. They tell us if a healthy child is at risk for depression in the future, whether weeks, months, or years away.

By understanding the risk factors for depression, you can do a great deal to help protect your child. You can more accurately determine if he is vulnerable, stay alert to warning signs and symptoms, and increase the chances of recognizing—and getting the best treatment for—problems early. And if your child is at risk but has not yet developed depression, you can take some preventive steps—which we'll discuss later on in this book—to help head off the problem before it begins.

Before we explore these risk factors, let me offer some advice: Try not to view them as absolutes. While I discuss each one individually—because that's the clearest way to explain risk factors—in real life there is a great deal of interplay among them. To a large extent, it is this interaction, combined with the biological, emotional, and social considerations we discussed in chapter 1, that determine whether or not your child will become depressed.

For example, a youngster will not necessarily become depressed if her parents get divorced, although divorce is a risk factor. Although she is more likely to become depressed than a child from a happy, intact family, she may be less at risk than a child from a divorced family that is filled with violence, tension, and discord. A child's vulnerability to depression depends on her experiences and on the environment in which she's lived.

Risk factors also have a cumulative effect. A child of divorce is at less risk for depression than a child of divorce who has also been abused. And that child may be less vulnerable than one who, on top of divorce and abuse, comes from a family with a history of depression.

Eleven Major Risk Factors for Depression

▪ Gender

Research shows that among young children, boys are more likely to be depressed than girls. In adolescence, the reverse holds true; studies suggest that by the time children reach their teenage years, girls are twice as likely as boys to become depressed. Teenage girls also tend to suffer from more severe depression and to have longer first episodes.

While this is the common wisdom, I believe such "facts" are misleading because they are colored by the differences in the way boys and girls express their depression and in the way we view their behavior. When young girls get depressed, for example, they are more likely to become withdrawn and quiet. But because we perceive this passive behavior as socially acceptable—that is, it's the way we *expect* "good" girls to behave—we don't necessarily suspect a problem, so the depression may go undetected.

When young boys get depressed, however, they often behave very differently. They frequently become disruptive, fight with classmates and siblings, disobey teachers and parents, and break rules or even laws. This defiant behavior draws attention to the child, and so he is more likely to get referred to a school guidance counselor or mental health professional. Since more young boys are referred for help, it stands to reason that more boys are diagnosed—which may explain why more young boys than girls are considered depressed.

This dynamic takes a different spin in adolescence when the research shows that depression affects more girls than boys. Although depressed girls' behavior doesn't change much—teenagers, like their younger counterparts, also tend to be quiet, withdrawn, and isolated— in adolescence this behavior is less socially acceptable; instead, it is associated with the classic symptoms of adult depression. So the problem is more likely to be detected and diagnosed.

Adolescent boys also continue to express their depression the way they did when they were younger, often becoming aggressive, argu- mentative, angry, sullen, or even violent. But at this stage, such behavior is more likely to get them disciplinary action than coun- seling, so that their depression often goes undetected or misdiag- nosed—which is why I believe it's misleading to assume that teenage girls are at greater risk for depression than teenage boys.

■ **Previous Depression**

Typically, depression is a chronic problem. Peter Lewinsohn, Ph.D., of the Oregon Research Institute in Eugene, has been following the same children—about 1,500 in total—for some ten years. And he's found that fully 44 percent of those who developed depression before age eighteen experienced another episode by the time they turned twenty-four. Other studies have shown recurrence rates of as high as 50 percent—which leads us to believe that *the greatest predictor of depression is a previous episode of depression.*

But does this mean that once your child becomes clinically depressed he is destined to suffer for the rest of his life?

Not at all. Because what the research and statistics don't take into account is efforts to identify and treat clinical depression. When depression is diagnosed early and accurately, and when it is treated effectively, you can significantly reduce the risk of recurrence. Through treatment, children can also learn to identify the feelings or thoughts that may signal an oncoming depression—"I'm starting to worry a lot about school" or "I don't have fun when I play with my friends anymore" or "It's getting hard for me to fall asleep at night"— and can learn to reach out to their parent or doctor *before* the depression becomes overwhelming.

Parents, too, can learn from experience in order to recognize children's early signs of depression—such as difficulty sleeping, falling grades, or loss of appetite—and give their kids the support they need. These tactics can help ward off a recurrence entirely or, at the very least, greatly temper its effects.

■ Family History

If you, your spouse, or other close relative has suffered from depression, your child is at increased risk. Research reveals that children with a depressed parent are twice as likely to develop depression as kids whose parents aren't depressed; if both parents have had depression, the risk quadruples. Studies also confirm that kids whose biological parents have had depression are at higher risk even if they were adopted at birth and raised by parents who have never been depressed.

Genetics also seems to affect the age at which depression might begin. Donna Moreau, M.D., clinical director of the Children's Anxiety and Depression Clinic of Columbia Presbyterian Medical Center in New York City, reports that if even one parent suffered from depression before he or she reached puberty, his or her child has a thirteen-fold greater chance of developing depression by the age of thirteen than a youngster whose parent was not depressed.

Studies of twins also support the importance of genetics. Research on identical twins—that is, twins who have the same genetic makeup—has shown that if one twin suffers from clinical depression, there is a 30 to 40 percent chance that the other will, too. Studies of nonidentical or fraternal twins—siblings who are no more genetically alike than other pairs of siblings—show a likelihood of about 15 to 20 percent. In other words, the closer your genetic tie to a depressed sibling or relative, the higher your risk factor for depression.

However, these findings don't diminish the importance of environment and experience. In fact, the very studies that point to genetics and biology as the basis for depression also provide proof that other factors are involved. If genetics were the sole cause of depression, then if one identical twin were depressed, the chance that the other twin would suffer depression would be 100 percent, not 30 to 40 percent as the research reveals.

■ Stressful Life Events

Life isn't evenhanded in doling out difficulties. Some kids must deal with traumatic events well before they are emotionally or intellectually ready. Parents die or divorce, a brother or sister falls seriously ill, a trusted adult becomes physically abusive. When children experience such stressful events, their risk for depression rises.

THE CODDINGTON SCALE

Are some life events more stressful than others? Absolutely, according to the Coddington Life Stress Scale, the best-known and most widely used life-stress measure for children. Developed by R. D. Coddington, M.D., the scale assigns numerical values to various life events at different points in childhood; the greater the stress, the higher the number assigned. These individual values are added together to get a cumulative stress figure. The higher the total, the more stress the child has experienced.

Let me emphasize that this scale is NOT a diagnostic tool for depression. But research suggests that the higher a child's score on the Coddington Scale, the greater the *likelihood* of depression.

Life Event	Preschool	Elementary	High School
Beginning school	42	46	42
Change to a different school	33	46	56
Birth or adoption of sibling	50	50	50
Brother or sister leaving home	39	36	37
Hospitalization of a sibling	37	41	41
Death of a sibling	59	68	68
Change of father's occupation requiring increased absence	36	45	38
Loss of job by parent	23	38	46
Marital separation of parents	74	78	69
Divorce of parents	74	84	77
Hospitalization or serious illness of parent	51	55	55
Death of parent	89	91	87
Death of grandparent	30	38	36
Marriage of parent to stepparent	62	65	63
Jail sentence of parent for thirty days or less	34	44	53
Jail sentence of parent for one year or more	67	67	75
Addition of third adult to family	39	41	34
Change in parent's financial status	21	29	45
Mother beginning work	47	44	26
Decrease in number of arguments between parents	21	25	27
Increase in number of arguments between parents	44	51	46
Decrease in number of arguments with parents	22	27	26
Increase in number of arguments with parents	39	47	47
Discovery of being an adopted child	33	52	64
Acquiring a visible deformity	52	69	81

Life Event	Preschool	Elementary	High School
Having a visible congenital deformity	39	60	62
Being hospitalized	59	62	58
Change in acceptance by peers	38	51	67
Outstanding personal achievement	23	39	46
Death of a close friend	38	53	63
Failure of a year in school		57	56
Suspension from school		46	50
Pregnancy of unwed teenage sister		36	64
Becoming involved with drugs or alcohol		61	76
Becoming a member of church/synagogue		25	31
Not making an extracurricular activity you wanted to be involved in (band, athletic team)		49	55
Breaking up with boyfriend or girlfriend		47	53
Beginning to date		55	51
Fathering an unwed pregnancy		76	77
Unwed pregnancy		95	92
Being accepted to a college of your choice			43
Getting married			101

The Coddington Scale provides a useful way for parents, clinicians, and researchers to compare how stressful certain life events are for children of different ages. For instance, Coddington's research shows that between the ages of four and six, the average total life stress score is about 75; the average score for children between nine and twelve is approximately 100, and between the ages of fourteen and sixteen, it may approach 200. If your child scores higher than these averages, he may be at greater risk for depression than you realized—which means you need to be particularly alert to depression's early warning signs and symptoms, all of which I'll discuss shortly.

Now not every situation listed on the Coddington Scale directly increases your child's vulnerability to depression. Remember, it's the *interaction* and *cumulative effect* of these factors that count most. But certain stressors are more influential than others in determining whether or not your child will get depressed. These are the ones that interfere with your child's sense of security, and with his belief that the world around him is relatively stable and secure. Without this solid foundation, it is hard for any child to develop the self-esteem, confidence, and resilience he needs to cope with life's everyday ups and downs, much less more traumatic experiences. Let's take a closer look at the stressful life events most closely linked with depression.

A SIGNIFICANT LOSS

Most kids encounter losses growing up, such as the death of a beloved pet, a friend who moves away, or the loss of only-child status when a baby brother or sister arrives. By and large, youngsters adjust to these situations well. But when children experience even more traumatic losses, their risk for depression is heightened. Among these, three stand out:

The Death of a Parent Children who lose a parent often suffer from periods of apathy, withdrawal, disturbed sleep and appetite, decreased energy, and anxiety. In short, the death of a parent can devastate a child. Unless the surviving parent or caregiver can give the child the love, support, and attention she needs, helping her build a sense of self-esteem, security, and self-worth, a child who loses a parent is at increased risk for depression.

Losses Linked to Parental Divorce Every year, over one million children are involved in a family divorce, according to the latest Census Bureau estimates. And these kids endure several losses. Most significant is the loss of the intact family the child has come to know. Another is the loss of, or changed relationship with, the noncustodial parent, which can leave a child forever wary of close relationships.

Divorce can also disrupt a child's social ties; if the custodial parent moves, the child often leaves family and friends behind. Even if the parent and child stay put, the youngster often loses touch with grandparents, aunts, uncles, and other members of the noncustodial parent's family.

Of course, not every divorce brings about such losses. Sometimes, the child often sees both parents, stays in contact with all his relatives, and remains in the same home, school, and town—all of which help to offset the stress of divorce. Unfortunately, however, such "cooperative" breakups are relatively rare and the losses that children typically suffer do leave them more vulnerable to depression.

The story of seven-year-old Adam is a case in point. Adam was referred to me because of his increasingly disruptive behavior. At school, he picked fights with the other kids, talked back to the teacher, and never turned in his homework. At home, he twice poured laundry detergent into the family fish tank, set a series of small fires in the backyard, and repeatedly tried to "kill" his baby sister's favorite doll by stabbing it over and over again with a penknife.

Attempting to handle the situation herself, Adam's mom read several popular parenting books, and over the course of several months tried the techniques they suggested. But when Adam's conduct continued to worsen, she contacted me.

During our first sessions together, Adam pounded the table, furiously shredded paper, and repeatedly smacked a punching bag. But after a while, his aggressive exterior gave way, revealing an extremely sad little boy. He confided that he was very unhappy about his parents' six-month-old divorce and felt that he was to blame. He also said he "hated" his dad's "dumb new girlfriend" and was upset because his father frequently missed scheduled visits. "My dad never shows up when he says. Then everyone gets mad and I feel bad all over," Adam said.

My initial interactions with Adam, combined with the intensity and duration of his symptoms, led me to conclude that he was clinically depressed. Short-term therapy provided Adam with a safe, supportive outlet for his anger, sadness, and frustration. We were also able to make arrangements so that his father's visits became much more predictable, although less frequent.

Within a few months, Adam was feeling better and his behavior began to improve. Now in the third grade, he has calmed down and seems a good deal happier. He continues to adjust to his parents' divorce, but he no longer feels responsible for the breakup. Joining a school-sponsored group created to help kids cope with divorce and remarriage has helped him realize that he's not alone, and that many other children have had similar experiences and feelings.

The Death of a Sibling Although not common, the death of a brother or sister is a devastating loss that greatly increases the risk of depression. One reason is that children experience survivor's guilt; they feel guilty that they are alive while their brother or sister is not. Some children may even feel responsible for their sibling's death. Surviving children also have a tough time coping with the reactions of their parents, who are often so consumed by their own grief that they have trouble giving their remaining youngsters the attention they need.

Sometimes parents idealize the deceased child in an effort to keep his memory alive. But this reaction can damage the surviving children's self-esteem; no matter now hard they try, they can never measure up to the memories of the deceased sibling. Without adequate love, understanding, and guidance to help them make this difficult emotional journey, surviving children are highly vulnerable to depression.

Take the case of Kelly. A generally happy energetic preschooler, her behavior changed dramatically after her baby sister died of SIDS (Sudden Infant Death Syndrome). Kelly had been very attached to the infant, helping her mom feed, change, and care for her. When the baby died, Kelly blamed herself, saying "One night, I heard the baby cry. But I didn't tell anyone. When I went into her room in the morning, she didn't wake up." After the baby was cremated, her parents put the ashes in an urn, which they kept on a shelf in the kitchen, a constant reminder to Kelly of her baby sister's death.

In the weeks that followed, Kelly became both self-destructive and aggressive. At bedtime, she would often bang her head against the headboard. She refused to brush her teeth, saying she wanted them to "rot out." Several times, she hit her parents and older brother. At day care, she would throw blocks and toys across the room, and overturn tables and chairs during group time.

With treatment—play therapy and antidepressant medication—Kelly was eventually able to overcome her emotional problems. (For a detailed discussion of these and other effective treatments, see chapter 8.) Now she is in the first grade and doing quite well. She has not had any recurrence of her depression. But her story highlights the powerful impact the death of a sibling can have on even a very young child.

DISASTERS

Other traumatic life events are brought about by natural or man-made disasters—a hurricane destroys a home, an earthquake demolishes the family business, a terrorist's bomb explodes near a day-care center. Such events can make a child more vulnerable to depression.

According to research conducted at UCLA by disaster experts Robert Pynoos, M.D., and Alan Steinberg, Ph.D., the risk of depression rises when children who experience a disaster endure continuing adversity. When these researchers studied children who survived the 1988 earthquake in Armenia, for example, they found that those who suffered severe economic hardships and family disruptions for months or even years afterward—the family home was destroyed and new housing could not be found, or the parents lost their jobs and income so the family didn't have enough food to eat—were much more likely to develop depression than those children whose lives were unsettled for only a short time.

MAJOR CHANGES IN THE CHILD'S ENVIRONMENT

Disasters that radically change a child's surroundings for a substantial period of time prevent that youngster from growing up in a safe, stable, and secure environment that helps protect him from depression. Other changes can have a similar effect.

Changing neighborhoods or schools can be quite stressful, particularly when the child moves to a place that's radically different from what he was used to—an inner-city child moves to a rural area, a youngster who spent years at a flexible, child-centered Montessori school is sent off to a strictly run boarding school. Such a transition can be very traumatic and heighten the youngster's vulnerability to depression.

Sometimes, a change in the family's finances can increase the risk for depression. If a parent loses a job and cannot find another, the family may be forced to move to a poorer neighborhood. On the other end of the spectrum, I knew a child whose life changed when his father won the lottery. The family moved from a middle-class neighborhood to an exclusive, wealthy community, and the child found himself ostracized by the children of "old-money" families. The youngster became sad, confused, and ultimately, clinically depressed.

In order for children to grow and develop normally, they must be willing and able to reach out and explore the world around them. But in order to do this, they need to know that they have a safe, secure home base to which they can return. When a stressful event severely and continuously disrupts that home base, the risk of depression rises.

■ Child Abuse

In 1995, over three million children were reported as victims of child abuse and neglect, according to the National Committee to Prevent Child Abuse. Repeated physical, sexual, or emotional abuse puts these children at high risk for depression because it prevents them from developing positive self-esteem and self-worth.

At the Anna Jaques Child Psychiatry Program at the Amesbury Health Center, a twelve-bed children's inpatient psychiatric hospital in Massachusetts, we see many children who have been abused. These children often believe that they are bad, worthless, and deserving of such abuse. The rage that abuse can generate in a child can turn her into a cruel and abusive bully or an extremely passive "victim" who views the world as a scary, unsafe place. Ongoing abuse also can make a child unable to tolerate any frustration. When disappointed, the youngster may fly into a tantrum or engage in self-destructive behavior driven by a sense of self-loathing and helplessness. It's no wonder, then, that abused children are at high risk for depression.

Another important point: If you were abused as a child, you are at greater risk of abusing your own children. If you fall into this category and ever feel that you are beginning to reenact the patterns from your own childhood, get help right away.

▪ Temperament

All babies are born with certain emotional traits. Some are charmingly social, smiling and cooing when approached, while others are timid, shying away from anyone but Mommy. Some infants cry at the slightest noise or sudden movement, while others regard such intrusions with surprise and curiosity. Some infants and toddlers are energetic and active; others are calm and placid. These traits form a child's temperament and create the emotional backdrop against which a youngster's personality and emotional makeup develop.

One of the most important aspects of temperament is adaptability. Children who have a high degree of adaptability, who adjust easily to unfamiliar or different situations—new foods, new baby, new school, or new home—seem to be better protected against depression. After being disappointed or frustrated, adaptable children may be sad for a while but quickly regain their emotional equilibrium. Kids who do not adapt easily, however, are more readily overwhelmed by stress and are more likely to cross the line between sadness and depression.

▪ Inconsistent or Unstable Caregiving

Inconsistent or unstable caregiving can make children more vulnerable to depression. This is important to understand, since the increase in single-parent and two-income families has had a dramatic effect on the growth of child care. According to a recent National Child Care Survey conducted by the Urban Institute, 63 percent of working mothers and 33 percent of at-home mothers use some form of supplemental child care. The survey estimates that over thirteen million children under the age of thirteen are currently in some form of supervised child care. By the year 2000, that number will top twenty million.

There's been a lot of discussion among professionals about the effect of early child care on children. Some experts believe that child care for kids under two may put them at risk for later social, behavioral, and emotional problems, including depression. Others disagree, citing research that shows that children who attend good-quality child-care programs turn out to be as emotionally healthy as children who are not in child care.

I believe that *high-quality* child care—that is, child care with low staff turnover, low child/caregiver ratio, well-trained and well-paid staff, and a safe, well-designed, stimulating environment with age-appropriate toys and equipment—can help children become confident, secure, and resilient, and can reduce their risk of depression and other emotional problems.

High-quality care can also benefit society. A few years ago, the High/Scope Perry Preschool study of an early-childhood program in Ypsilanti, Michigan, found that for every dollar invested in high-quality early-childhood care, we get seven dollars back in savings, such as in programs geared to help troubled youth.

Young children need consistent and predictable relationships with all the caregivers in their lives. When children are pulled in and out of various child-care settings, it hinders the development of trust, self-esteem, and coping skills. Clearly, multiple or disrupted relationships with caregivers make children more vulnerable to depression.

Abbey's story is a poignant example. An attractive, soft-spoken thirty-one-year-old artist, Abbey has suffered from low self-esteem and recurrent depression throughout her life. After years of therapy, she is only now beginning to feel good about herself. In researching this book, I spent time talking with her about the roots of her problem. Here's what she said.

"My happiest moments were when I was very little. My mother would read Grimm's fairy tales to me at bedtime and take me to the bookmobile. But when I was about four or five—we were living in Mississippi because my father, who was an army recruit, was stationed there—my dad left to fight in Vietnam. He never came back. So my mother had to find a job so support us. It took awhile, but she finally found a job in sales for a local manufacturing company.

"That's when she started traveling a lot. Sometimes she'd be gone for several weeks at a time, and I was left with a series of baby-sitters—some nice, some not. I remember that the rules were always changing; one sitter would want things one way, then she'd leave and another sitter would want things another way. And then when my mom's income would drop off because she had a bad sales month, she'd fire whichever baby-sitter I had at the moment and leave me with one of her many relatives. Even when my mom came home, things weren't predictable. Sometimes, she'd have lots of energy and pay lots of attention to me, and other times she'd be so exhausted that she'd just go to bed. It was all very confusing.

"I was about seven when my depression began. I can remember sitting out on a nearby pier, looking at the lights over the bay, and feeling so lost and sad. I was brought up Catholic, and I remember praying a lot, saying to God, 'I'll be really good if you'll just help me.' I felt really sad; I didn't feel like I had any place to turn. I loved my mom, but I could never depend on her."

I asked Abbey how she thought her depression had affected her life.

"I feel I've missed a lot. Relationships have always been hard for me; I've been afraid to get close, so I've picked men who were very unavailable emotionally. I'm okay though, thanks to some close friends and therapy. I've moved ahead with my life. But I always think that if someone—my mom or some other adult—had been there for me consistently, I could have been so much happier because I would have felt so much more secure and safe."

■ Problems Between Mom and Dad

Children living in homes in which there is persistent tension between the parents are at higher risk for depression than children in less troubled environments. One reason is that the battling parents get so involved in their disputes that they neglect the needs of their kids. Another is that the parents often make children the focus of their arguments, which can make the youngsters feel guilty, angry, and resentful.

It doesn't seem to matter if the children are actually at the center of the disputes; kids tend to blame themselves anyway. A preschooler may become convinced that Mom and Dad are angry because "I left my toys all over the living room." An older child may believe that his poor grades are upsetting his parents. Once again, the guilt and shame children feel can hamper their healthy emotional growth.

And don't think you can hide this conflict from the kids; children always pick it up. They are surprisingly sensitive to the actions, reactions, and interactions of the people around them. I've had parents tell me, "We never argue in front of the kids." But when I speak to the children, they say, "Mom and Dad have been fighting with each other for six months."

■ Drug and Alcohol Abuse

Substance abuse raises a child's risk for depression in several ways. If the parent is the abuser, it affects his ability to be consistent with his child. One day Dad's fine—patient, cheerful, and loving—and the next day he's irritable, critical, and distant. This unpredictability is confusing to children, and they grow up without the sense of stability and security so necessary to protect themselves against depression.

Parents who abuse drugs and alcohol are also more likely to abuse their children and cause all the emotional damage that we've already discussed. What's more, many times parents who abuse drugs or alcohol are depressed and trying to medicate themselves in order to deal with their emotional pain. They may not realize that they are clinically depressed and that their own depression raises their children's risk.

Drugs and alcohol may also disguise depression in children—especially teenagers—who, like many adults, are abusing these substances not merely to "get high" but as a way of dulling painful emotions and helping themselves feel normal again. Parents, teachers, and other caregivers need to remember, then, that the underlying cause of children's substance abuse may well be depression.

■ Poor Social Skills/Unpopularity

Children who are isolated, unpopular, or labeled "different" by their peers are at higher risk for depression than children who are socially adept. These unpopular kids may behave badly—like the young bully who knocks down the other kids' sand castle—in order to get the attention they crave. Such behavior reinforces that child's social isolation and, as the cycle continues, the youngster often develops serious problems with self-esteem and becomes more likely to get depressed.

■ Illness in the Family

Parental illness becomes a significant risk factor only when it prevents Mom or Dad from spending time with and remaining emotionally available to their children. If you have a condition that demands repeated hospitalizations and long absences, your youngsters may be at greater risk for depression.

The serious illness of a sibling can also place your other children at risk, particularly if you allow it to consume *all* your time and attention. The healthy youngsters can become jealous, angry, or sad, believing that their parents are ignoring them because they've done something wrong or because they're "bad" or in some way unworthy.

■ A Mix of Factors

The many risk factors we've just explored rarely occur in isolation from one another. Most of the time, several factors come together in a child's life and make him vulnerable to depression. And often, the depression that begins in childhood continues, on and off, throughout adulthood or at least until the problem is accurately diagnosed and properly treated.

An important reminder: Having a child who is at *risk* for depression doesn't mean that he will necessarily develop the problem. Some children seem to have a natural resiliency that protects them; others need your help in developing such emotional adaptability—I'll explain how later on. But there is hope. In almost all cases, depression can be either prevented or treated successfully so that these children can enjoy full, happy lives.

Chapter

3

Is Your Child Depressed?

How to Spot the Signs and Symptoms

When I get depressed, I feel mixed up. My face feels flat, like I can't smile, no matter what.

—Melissa, age eleven

Children typically go through some very trying stages as they grow up. The outgoing preschooler may suddenly become fearful and shy; the on-the-go nine-year-old may now want to spend all his time at his computer; the easygoing twelve-year-old turns thirteen and suddenly perceives every event in her life—from tearing her favorite blouse to losing a class election—as a major crisis. Usually, though, these are just phases, and eventually children grow out of them.

Sometimes, however, an abrupt change in your child's behavior or manner is more than a passing stage; instead, it can be a symptom of a serious emotional problem like depression.

Depression isn't easy to identify in children. In fact, until the early eighties when it was recognized as a true disorder, even professionals often missed it. One reason was that our understanding of childhood depression was shaped by our knowledge of depression in adults. So unless we saw the same intense sadness and tearfulness in a child, or knew that the youngster experienced feelings of worthlessness and hopelessness, we did not suspect depression.

Now we realize that children, who are just learning how to express the many emotions they feel, may communicate their distress very differently from adults. Very young children who don't yet have the verbal skills to put their feelings into words may never say "I'm feeling down" or "I feel like there's no hope left." Instead, they often act out their upset by behaving in ways that look very unlike what we think of as "depression." But a child who bullies his baby sister, picks fights at school, or suddenly suffers frequent and unexplained aches and pains may be expressing his depression just as surely as the child who becomes tearful and withdrawn.

Another thing that makes spotting depression difficult is that as children grow and develop, their symptoms often change. So the behaviors that might flag depression in your preschooler are not necessarily the same ones that could signal a problem in your teenager. Five-year-old Brandon's playground brawling looks very different from fifteen-year-old Jennifer's cutting school and "zoning out" in front of the TV every afternoon, but both behaviors could be symptomatic of depression.

Research confirms the many variations in the symptoms of childhood depression. In one 1987 study, researchers at the University of Pittsburgh and the New York State Psychiatric Institute found that younger kids who were depressed complained of physical problems like stomachaches and restlessness, experienced great anxiety when separated from their parents or caregivers, and developed fears of places and situations. Depressed adolescents, however, typically showed other symptoms; they tended to sleep more, feel hopeless, experience a weight change, or abuse drugs.

You also need to take a child's age into account. A two-year-old who frequently cries or screams for attention may be behaving quite normally for her age, but an eight-year-old who does the same thing is probably telling you that he's in emotional pain.

As we discussed in chapter 2, temperament also influences how children's depression may look. Every baby is born with a certain temperament; some are affectionate and cheerful, others more somber and placid, still others active and mischievous. As a baby develops, his temperament forms the basis of his personality and influences the ways in which he will cope with life. For example, a baby who smiles and coos a great deal gets many grins in return. As he matures, he learns that smiling will get him what he wants—whether that's a hug from his mom or the undivided attention of his preschool teacher. So smiling and being cheerful becomes an important part of how he interacts with others and copes with the world. If a temperamentally irritable toddler discovers that whimpering brings him what he wants, whining and complaining may become an important aspect of his personality style as he gets older.

The time to pay extra attention, however, is when your child's personality suddenly changes. If your affectionate six-year-old abruptly starts refusing your hugs and kisses, pulling away whenever you reach out and touch him, your parenting antennae should go up; something's probably amiss. But if he has never been particularly cuddly, squirming and crawling off your lap as a baby and refusing to hold your hand as a toddler, pulling away now doesn't necessarily mean anything's wrong.

The story of nine-year-old Julie illustrates this idea. An engaging, outgoing child who always had lots of friends around her, Julie did well at school and seemed quite happy. But about three weeks before her ninth birthday, she told her mom and dad that she didn't want a party. Her parents were taken by surprise; Julie had always loved her birthday celebrations, looking forward to them with unabashed enthusiasm. But her parents respected her wishes and instead remembered her birthday with a quiet family dinner.

The next month, they got a note from Julie's teacher that read, "She used to be so eager, always raising her hand and volunteering for projects. But for the past several weeks, that's stopped. She doesn't seem to be putting her usual energy into her work. Is there something happening at home that may be affecting her?"

That night, Julie's parents spoke with their daughter, but she only replied, "Well, school's boring. The work's dumb." They encouraged her to try harder, but since Julie had always been such a trouble-free child, they chalked up her attitude to a phase and didn't give the matter too much more thought.

It wasn't until several weeks later that her parents really became concerned. One night at dinner, Julie said she wasn't hungry and asked to be excused. She went to her room and closed the door. About an hour later, Julie's mom heard her quietly sobbing. When she asked her daughter what was wrong, Julie answered, "I feel like I'm no good, like everything I do comes out wrong. I try to make it better, but I can't." Her mom tried to see if something had happened to trigger such feelings, but Julie couldn't point to anything specific.

Julie's parents spoke with her pediatrician and school counselor; both felt that she should be seen by a child psychiatrist, which is how she came to me. As I worked with her, I learned that her sadness had not started suddenly; actually, she'd been feeling down for months. She'd also had trouble sleeping and rarely felt hungry. When I checked with her pediatrician, he said her weight had dropped below what was normal for her size and age. She'd also lost interest in the activities she used to enjoy, particularly skating in the park with her friends.

Julie's sad feelings didn't appear to be caused by any specific event. They seemed "global," that is, they were affecting many areas of her life and had been going on for several months. Julie, I believed, was clinically depressed.

I considered treating her with antidepressants, but because she seemed so eager to feel better, "to be happy again," as she put it, I felt that she might be able to improve without medication. She and I worked in one-on-one therapy where she had a safe place to express her fears and frustrations. At the same time, we worked out a program with her teachers to help them give Julie more positive feedback and encouragement, like noticing and praising her work and accomplishments. I felt this increased attention would help build Julie's self-esteem. Finally, I helped her parents learn how to encourage Julie to vent her feelings and to feel good about herself.

Within four weeks, we saw significant improvement. Julie was feeling happier, sleeping better, and enjoying skating again. Within three months, she was back to her normal self. Two years later, she has had no recurrence of her depression.

Why Early Detection Is Important

Depression usually occurs in time-limited periods. Even without treatment, the average episode of major depression ends within about nine months.

But that doesn't mean that depression should be left to run its course. On the contrary, allowing the problem to go untreated threatens a child's emotional health and well-being for several reasons. First, as we've already discussed, the recurrence rate of untreated depression is very high; as many as 50 percent of children with untreated depression suffer another episode within three years. Second, the longer the initial episode goes ignored, the sooner the next will occur.

Untreated depression also can create severe emotional and developmental setbacks. A depressed child is less likely to make friends, do well in school, join clubs, participate in sports, or get involved in other activities that help develop healthy self-esteem and important life skills. Without a strong self-image and good coping skills, a child is much more likely to suffer recurring emotional and social problems with long-lasting consequences.

One of the best ways I know to explain the repercussions of untreated depression is to offer the story of Tom, a fifty-one-year-old postal clerk I interviewed in researching this book. His compelling story illustrates the difficulties that can arise over the course of a lifetime for a child whose depression goes undetected and untreated.

"I always felt different from the other kids, even when I was as young as three or four," Tom recalls. "By the time I was six, I'd grown painfully shy; I have a distinct memory of standing in a playground and crying because I wanted to play with the other kids but I just couldn't connect with them. I did have a kitten that I cared for, but it died. And I remember not being able to grieve for it or to talk about my feelings. That's something we didn't do in my family.

"My maternal grandfather was always very sad, and my mother was, too. My father was perpetually angry and a very isolated person. I grew up surrounded by people who just couldn't nurture me, so I always felt like an unhappy outsider. Gradewise, I did okay in elementary and

high school. But once I got to college, I couldn't study; I couldn't orga-
nize my thoughts. All I could feel was this deep-down sadness. So I
dropped out."

Many unhappy years followed, but it wasn't until Tom reached his
late thirties that he saw a psychiatrist who diagnosed his problem as
depression and treated him with antidepressant medication and
psychotherapy. Fairly quickly, Tom's life changed dramatically.

"I felt like Rip Van Winkle; after nearly twenty-five years of sleeping
through my life, I was waking up. I started to laugh again—I hadn't
laughed since junior high school! If I'd only gotten help earlier, my life
would have been very different. If I were to give advice to any parent,
I'd tell them to pay attention to their kids when they're young. If
they're depressed, don't ignore it. There's help out there. *Please* find it."

How to Tell If Your Child Is Depressed

What's the best way to tell if your child is depressed? I recommend a
four-pronged approach:

- *First, know your child well.* Be involved with the various aspects of her
  life so that you'll be more likely to notice any changes in behavior or
  demeanor that may signal an emotional problem.
- *Second, learn all you can about the symptoms of depression.* This
  heightened awareness will help you recognize warning signs should
  they appear in your child.
- *Third, if you suspect your child is depressed, make sure you rule out
  physical problems that may be causing her symptoms.* Recognizing
  depression isn't easy, particularly since behaviors or moods that
  appear to be depression may turn out to be something very different
  indeed.

    Take Jenna, for example. An active, popular, and confident young-
    ster who earned a solid B average at school, at age fourteen she
    became increasingly sluggish, oversleeping every morning and going
    to her room to nap right after school. Also, her grades began to slip. "I
    just can't seem to concentrate any more," she complained to her

mom, who noticed that her daughter had become very irritable, a dramatic change from her previously cheerful disposition.

One of Jenna's teachers suspected depression and suggested that her parents take her to see a local child and adolescent psychiatrist. The doctor's detailed interview with Jenna and her parents included a comprehensive history of her early development, childhood illnesses, and recent symptoms. Based on that information and a consultation with Jenna's pediatrician, he ordered a series of blood tests, which revealed the problem: an underactive thyroid. Jenna was placed on thyroid medication; within a few weeks, her "depressive" symptoms disappeared completely.

The lesson is clear: Even when you suspect depression, first make sure that any physical causes are completely ruled out.

- *Fourth, trust your instincts.* Most parents are wonderfully accurate at sensing when something's wrong with their youngster. If you've ruled out physical causes but still think there's a problem, consult a mental health professional; only someone who is well trained in children's emotional issues can accurately diagnose clinical depression in your child. (See chapter 7 for advice on how to choose the right therapist.)

■ The Choate Depression Inventory for Children

Back in chapter 1, I mentioned that the best way to figure out if your child might be depressed is to ask yourself to what extent his feelings and behavior interfere with his everyday life and normal development. To answer this question more fully, take a look at the following questionnaire. It's called the Choate Depression Inventory for Children (CDIC), and I designed it to help the children and parents we work with at Choate spot the earliest signs of depression. Please note that the questionnaire is an adaptation and expansion of several other surveys currently used in research and clinical practice; it is *not* a formal research tool or diagnostic test. But going through the items will help you become aware of the symptoms of depression and recognize them in your child.

I suggest you use the CDIC in either of two ways. If your child is quite young and not yet very verbal, read through the True/False statements yourself and answer them as you think your child would. If your child is older and able to talk with you about these subjects, sit down and go through the questionnaire together. Explain what you're doing by saying something like "I was reading this book and it had a list of things kids worry about. Let's look at it together."

The Choate Depression Inventory for Children (CDIC)

Answer true or false.

	True	False
1. I feel sad lots of the time.	____	____
2. I have trouble sleeping.	____	____
3. I feel tired lots of the time.	____	____
4. I don't have many friends.	____	____
5. I cry a lot.	____	____
6. I don't like playing with other kids.	____	____
7. I don't feel as hungry as I used to.	____	____
8. Other kids don't like me.	____	____
9. I feel lonely.	____	____
10. I have lots of headaches and stomachaches.	____	____
11. I don't like school.	____	____
12. I have bad dreams.	____	____
13. Sometimes I think about hurting myself.	____	____
14. I worry a lot.	____	____
15. I don't like myself.	____	____
16. Other kids have more fun than I do.	____	____
17. I don't do as well in school as I used to.	____	____
18. Sometimes I have trouble concentrating.	____	____
19. I feel angry lots of the time.	____	____
20. I get into lots of fights.	____	____

If your child answers—or if you think your child would answer—"true" to three or more items, she should be evaluated by a qualified mental health professional; she may be clinically depressed. And if she answers "true" to item 13, which reveals self-destructive or suicidal thoughts, she should be evaluated immediately to ensure her physical safety.

The Signs and Symptoms of Clinical Depression

Before we detail the signs of clinical depression, I want to review four important points.

1. *No single symptom, in isolation, signals depression.* Remember, depression is best understood as a cluster of symptoms that together may indicate that your child is depressed.

2. *Symptoms must represent a noticeable change from the way your child usually acts.*

3. *Symptoms must be present for an extended period of time, generally at least two weeks.* They may be continuous or may come and go. Any normal child may be tearful and withdrawn for a day or two, particularly if she is reacting to a specific upsetting event, like being turned down for the lead in the school play. But if the tearfulness and isolation persist for several weeks or recur frequently, your child may be not just sad but clinically depressed.

4. *Symptoms must interfere with your child's everyday activities.* For instance, if your inveterate Little Leaguer starts missing games because he's "too tired" to play, he may have a problem.

What Is Bipolar Disorder?

Bipolar disorder, also known as manic depressive illness, is a condition in which individuals experience periods of depression as well as episodes of mania. Mania is characterized by feelings of increased energy, and an elevated or irritable mood accompanied by a combination of symptoms that may include:

- grandiosity
- pressured or rapid speech
- racing thoughts
- decreased need for sleep
- distractibility
- hyperactivity
- impulsive or risky behavior

True manic episodes are very rare in young children, although the incidence increases during adolescence. Research also suggests that some children who experience an episode of depression will go on to develop bipolar disorder later in life. The risk is much higher when there is also a family history of bipolar disorder.

Bipolar disorder in adults is a well-recognized condition with established and effective approaches to treatment. But research on the accurate diagnosis, treatment, and long-term prognosis for bipolar disorder in children is only now beginning to emerge. Someday, we may be better able to predict which of the children who experience depression are most likely to develop this illness. We may even learn how to prevent manic episodes altogether. For now, if your child experiences symptoms of mania and/or there is a history of bipolar disorder in your family, you will want to share this information with your child's clinician; it may have a significant effect on any diagnosis and treatment plans.

Fortunately, however, the majority of depressed kids will never experience a manic episode. With that in mind, let's focus on learning how to recognize depression at different stages in a child's development.

Depression in Infants and Toddlers

Babies experience a wide range of emotions, from happiness, surprise, and interest to anger, frustration, and sadness. Almost from birth, your baby becomes greatly attached to you, his primary caregiver, which is why crying, sulking, or other signs of sadness and protest are to be expected when your infant is separated from you, even for just an hour.

A strong bond between you and your child is healthy. It allows your youngster to develop his natural sense of curiosity, and his growing desire for independence and autonomy. As long as he knows he has a secure, loving caregiver to return to, he can venture out and explore the world around him. In fact, the healthy, normal toddler often becomes angry, sad, and frustrated by any attempts to limit his investigations and may cry or scream in protest when you stop him from exploring the light socket with his fingers or climbing on top of the refrigerator.

Most mental health professionals consider depression in infants and toddlers to be a form of "attachment disorder;" that is, the bond, or attachment, between an infant and his parent (or other important adult in his life) is either not well established or disturbed in some way. For example, a two-year-old I worked with became depressed when his grandmother, who was his primary caregiver, retired and moved across the country and the youngster was left in the care of a series of well-intentioned but inexperienced baby-sitters.

The story of baby Christina is another good example. Christina was born to a sixteen-year-old unwed mother named Angela. Because the baby's father assumed no responsibility for the child and Angela wanted to finish high school, mother and baby lived with Angela's parents. For a while, the baby seemed to be doing well, but at about nine months of age, her weight began to level off and soon fall well below normal. Although Christina had been fairly alert and responsive, she became more and more difficult to engage, often gazing into the distance when her grandmother, who took care of the child, tried to interest her with a brightly colored rattle or toy.

Christina's pediatrician became increasingly alarmed by her failure to thrive. He'd not found anything physically wrong with the baby and urged Angela and her mother to bring Christina to see me for a psychiatric evaluation.

Because Christina was so young, I worked extensively with the whole family. At the very first session, I noticed that Angela never interacted with her baby; instead, she sat alone, head down, at the far end of my office. During a subsequent session, she remarked, "My baby doesn't even know I'm her mother. It's like there's only room for one mother in this house, and it's not me." True enough. At every session, the grandmother held the baby, although not very tenderly. In fact, she often seemed angry at the infant and once told me she believed Christina soiled her diapers "on purpose, just to get at me."

As I worked with the family, it became clear that Angela and her baby were depressed. I suggested individual therapy for Angela, prescribed an antidepressant, and helped her enroll in a parenting class for teenage moms. Within several weeks, Angela seemed less withdrawn and became more active in mothering her baby. At the same time, I worked with the grandmother to help her give up the role of sole caregiver and instead to teach Angela how to to care for her baby herself. By the time Christina was fourteen months old, she had started gaining weight, was more interested and alert, and seemed to be on a more normal, healthy course. The family still had a long and difficult road ahead, but at least now they were going in the right direction.

Like little Christina, depressed babies often show several symptoms. In 1994, Washington, D.C.'s National Center for Clinical Infant Programs, in a publication called the *Diagnostic Classification of Mental Health and Developmental Disorders of Infancy and Early Childhood (DC: 0–3)*, developed this list of symptoms associated with depression in infants and very young children. According to the manual, infants and toddlers are depressed if, for a period of at least two weeks, they show the following:

- a pattern of depressed or irritable mood with diminished interest and/or pleasure in developmentally appropriate activities
- diminished capacity to protest
- excessive whining
- a diminished repertory of social interactions and decreased initiative

(Note: Any of these symptoms may be accompanied by disturbances in sleep or eating, including weight loss.)

This clinical, albeit bare-bones description of depression is useful, particularly for therapists looking for specific diagnostic guidelines. But the following additional symptoms—or in some cases, more fleshed-out descriptions of symptoms—will help alert you to the possibility of depression in your baby or toddler:

- *Sad or emotionless facial expression.* Healthy infants show a range of facial expressions: they frown, smile, grin, and appear wide-eyed and curious. Depressed children aren't very emotive; instead, their faces tend to be passive and unexpressive.
- *Little motor activity.* Healthy infants are active; they grasp with their hands, wiggle their feet, put their fist and other objects in their mouths, squirm in your arms, crawl, begin to pull themselves up, and finally, walk. Depressed babies tend to lie or sit in one place passively for relatively long periods of time and seem less eager to grasp at things or to get themselves up and moving.
- *Unresponsiveness or apathy; withdrawal.* Normal babies respond easily; they're quickly engaged by your speech, tone of voice, colorful toys or shiny objects, pictures books, and music. Depressed children are difficult to engage in play and often look away from you unresponsively. They may also babble less and, as they get older, may be less verbally expressive. Depressed toddlers may not show much curiosity in the people and things around them and often display little desire to master new tasks.
- *Excessive or unusually little crying.* Healthy babies and toddlers burst into brief paroxysms of tears a few times a day. Depressed children tend to cry either much more—or much less, although they frequently seem sad.
- *Failure to thrive.* Babies should grow and gain weight steadily from infancy throughout childhood. To help track their health, a pediatrician will measure babies' progress on a growth chart. Infants who fail to stay within the normal range—or whose pattern of growth suddenly drops off—will be closely evaluated and monitored. To be sure, there are many physical reasons for inadequate growth, such as poor nutrition or a problem with the infant's metabolism. But if the doctor finds no physical causes, it may be an emotional problem like depression that is causing this failure to thrive.

- *Frequent physical complaints.* Most babies and toddlers get sick from time to time, suffering occasional colds, sore throats, diarrhea, headaches, or tummy aches. But depressed children tend to have frequent troubles without any apparent cause.
- *Verbal expression of sadness.* Most toddlers have the verbal ability to express their pleasure or dismay. If your youngster tells you she's sad and doesn't know why, she may be suffering from depression.
- *Lack of social interest.* Older infants and toddlers usually like to play with other children. A youngster who sits off by himself while the other kids are playing may well be depressed.

One important note: Sometimes you'll notice minor forms of many of these symptoms in children who are not clinically depressed but who are reacting to stressful or changed circumstances in their lives, such as being malnourished or neglected, or having to adjust to a new caregiver when a parent returns to work. The difference is that in a nondepressed child, these symptoms disappear quickly once the situation is corrected—that is, when the baby gets enough to eat, receives sufficient care and attention, or simply gets used to his new caregiver. But a depressed child's symptoms will be persistent and severe, interfering with her normal emotional growth and development. That child should be seen by a mental health professional.

At a Glance: Symptoms of Depression in Infants and Toddlers

- Decreased pleasure in activities that should interest a child of this age and developmental level
- Sad or deadpan facial expression
- Little motor activity
- Withdrawal
- Too little or too much crying
- Excessive whining
- Failure to grow and thrive
- Verbal expressions of sadness
- Lack of social interest

Depression in Preschoolers

Normal, healthy three- to five-year-olds are active and curious. They're also highly egocentric, believing that they are the center of their world. Preschoolers are capable of expressing many intense emotions, from joy and delight to anger and sadness. When confronted by an upsetting situation, such as the death of an adored pet, preschoolers often feel true grief. They may cry, whine, experience some physical problems like stomachaches or headaches, suffer nightmares or disrupted sleep, or even regress to behaviors they've already outgrown, such as bed-wetting, thumb sucking, clinginess, or playing with baby toys. But this reaction is usually short-lived.

When a child is clinically depressed, these "symptoms" are not so brief; instead, they last for several weeks, although they may not be continuous. That is, they may appear, disappear, and reappear repeatedly over a given time period. Unfortunately, however, adults don't usually "read" these symptoms as depression, so the child's problem often goes unrecognized.

I was called to consult on a case at a local child-care center where Shannon, age three, was biting her peers and caregivers several times each day. (Occasional biting is not unusual for younger children, but by this age, the behavior is outside of the norm.) Her teachers were concerned not only about the unprovoked biting but about how so many negative interactions (constantly disciplining and saying "no" to Shannon, seeing other children refuse to play with her) would affect the little girl's self-esteem. For example, on several occasions Shannon would grab toys from classmates while exclaiming "Mine!" At other times, she would march over and intentionally knock down the block towers other children were carefully constructing.

As I observed Shannon, I noticed that she spent large amounts of time off in a corner by herself, wrapped in her "blankey," sucking her thumb, and watching the other children play. I also observed that although her speech was certainly developed, her vocabulary and language skills were not up to the level of her peers.

Both of Shannon's parents worked: her father was an administrator at a local hospital where her mother was a nurse. Shannon's mom had only just returned to nursing; she'd taken a few years off to stay home with Shannon and several months more when she became pregnant with Patrick, born just nine weeks earlier. Day care was Shannon's first real separation from her family.

Both parents felt they understood why Shannon was biting so much. Her mother said, "Clearly, she's mad because she's at day care now and she'd rather be with me." Her dad explained, "I think she's frustrated because she's very bright and has a lot of ideas but has difficulty expressing them all."

While they both made good points, further discussion uncovered several stressors in young Shannon's life. In addition to having to separate from her mom and losing her only-child status to her new brother, Shannon and her family recently had moved to a larger home, and a live-in nanny was hired to care for Patrick. What's more, the hospital where Shannon's parents worked had begun downsizing, and her mother and father were worried about losing their jobs. Given all the expenses they had recently taken on—the baby, Shannon's day care, Patrick's nanny, and the new house—the tension between Shannon's parents was high.

Since Shannon's pediatrician had ruled out any physical problems, I concluded that her depression was a reaction to the many losses and changes in her life. She was expressing her depressed feelings by biting and being aggressive. I recommended a treatment plan that included couples therapy for Shannon's parents (so that they could address the issues and stresses in their marriage) and introducing more consistency into Shannon's life, including scheduled meals and baths, and regular time alone with each parent. I also helped Shannon's child-care providers develop a reinforcement program to reward the youngster for not biting and to help her find other, more appropriate ways to express her feelings, like pounding on clay. Shannon and I worked one-on-one in short-term play therapy, where our use of puppets and play figures allowed her to give vent to her angry and sad feelings in less destructive ways. We also played games and read some of Shannon's favorite stories. Through these sessions, I became another point of consistency and predictability in Shannon's life, which helped her feel that the world around her was more secure and stable.

Within six months, Shannon was showing considerable improvement. While the biting had not disappeared completely, she was beginning to play with the other children in her day-care program. Her mood also improved considerably and, in general, she was becoming a happier child.

Shannon's story illustrates only some of the symptoms depressed children exhibit. Here are several others.

- *Physical complaints.* Preschoolers tend to bring home a variety of ailments, particularly when they're in contact with lots of other kids. But depressed preschoolers tend to suffer frequent and unexplained physical complaints such as stomachaches, headaches, diarrhea, and being "too tired to play."
- *Overactivity or underactivity.* While healthy preschoolers are usually active, depressed children may seem as if they're constantly in motion, unable to sit still or play quietly for even short periods of time. On the other hand, depressed children can seem sluggish, withdrawn, and generally less active than their peers.
- *A sad appearance.* One of the most endearing traits of preschoolers is their quick grin and the twinkle in their eyes. In contrast, depressed kids often have sad expressions characterized by downcast eyes, sagging lips, and furrowed brows, and they may smile only occasionally and fleetingly.
- *Low tolerance for frustration.* Depressed children often have a tough time dealing with even mild frustration and will frequently react with short outbursts of crying, screaming, or hitting. Frequent, full-blown temper tantrums, or a noticeable increase in tantruming, can also signal depression.
- *Irritability.* Any overtired child can become cranky. But depressed children often seem irritable even when they are not worn out.
- *Loss of pleasure in previously fun activities.* All kids outgrow certain activities. The video that delighted your child when he was two will probably bore him when he's four. But a sudden apathy toward a

favorite activity—a child who loves to paint or draw now refuses to participate in art projects; a youngster who adores jigsaw puzzles now stares listlessly at the pieces before him—may mean he's depressed.

- *Portraying the world as sad and bleak.* Preschoolers often express their feelings by drawing, so sketching a sad picture or two is perfectly normal when your child is feeling down. But when sad themes repeat themselves, you need to pay extra attention. One depressed six-year-old I worked with drew a picture of a solitary house—no trees, no grass, no people, no sun, no sky—and explained that "all the people have moved away. The house is sad and lonely."

At a Glance: Symptoms of Depression in Preschoolers

- Frequent, unexplained stomachaches, headaches, and fatigue
- Overactivity or excessive restlessness
- Frequent sadness
- Low tolerance for frustration
- Irritability
- Loss of pleasure in previously enjoyable activities
- Tendency to portray the world as sad or bleak

Depression in School-Aged Children

Once they reach school age, children become less egocentric and are able to see things from another's point of view. They can be quite sympathetic and empathetic, particularly toward other kids who may be crying or having a difficult time. By the time they are around eight years old, most kids are capable of understanding fairly abstract concepts.

School-aged children tend to move away from magical "there's a monster under the bed" fears and into more reality-based anxieties. They may worry about passing a spelling test, being accepted by their peers, or having their house blown away by an approaching tornado.

This developmental maturity helps explain why school-aged children are more likely than younger kids to have clinical depression. What's more, if your child has ever suffered from clinical depression in the past, she is more likely to get depressed as she gets older, especially if her initial depression wasn't diagnosed or treated.

Sometimes, though, a school-aged child becomes depressed for no apparent reason. This was the case with ten-year-old Mason. Mason was always a bit of a loner, although he had one or two close friends at school. He was very involved with computers and kept up on all the latest software. He also loved watching football, and since his dad's company had box seats, he frequently attended games with his father. So when Mason suddenly said he'd didn't "feel like" going to the game one Sunday, his parents took notice.

They also thought it strange when Mason decided not to accept his best friend's invitation to join in his family's trip to Disney World, a place Mason had been begging his parents to visit. But it wasn't until he began ignoring his computer that his mom and dad really started worrying.

First, they brought Mason to their pediatrician to see if he had "some kind of virus," but she could find nothing wrong. A few days later, Mason confided to his mother: "I just feel really sad all the time and I don't know why. I keep messing things up. And I'm no good at anything." His mother tried to reason with him, pointing out all the things Mason did well, but that didn't help. All he said was, "Well, you have to say that 'cause you're my mom."

At that point, Mason's pediatrician referred the family to me. During my initial interview with the child, he told me that he had been having trouble sleeping for months, that he "never felt hungry anymore" and that he had "problems keeping my mind straight at school." Although his symptoms clearly suggested depression, I didn't detect any particular trigger; he'd experienced no recent loss or change in his life or family situation. The only clue I had was when his father told me that when Mason was about seven, he'd gone through a period of several months when he was acting "very irritable" and "crying at the drop of a hat." As Mason's dad said, "He sort of withdrew from the family, but we thought it was just a phase. And after a while, he did seem to grow out of it." My guess was that Mason had suffered an earlier episode of depression, and since the problem had gone untreated, he was at increased risk for subsequent bouts, such as the one he was now experiencing.

I began to see Mason in individual therapy. I also started him on antidepressant medication. Within three weeks, many of his symptoms started to improve: he was sleeping better and his appetite had returned. In our sessions together, we focused on supporting his self-esteem and accepting the idea that feeling sad was not his fault because his depression was an illness, not a weakness. Over many games of checkers and Nerf basketball, we talked about his school and family life, and, gradually, his hopes and fears about the future. As is true with all my young patients, I let Mason be my guide during our sessions, trusting that the most important issues would eventually emerge. My job was to recognize the themes, point out connections, and offer helpful observations.

Within eight weeks, Mason had regained his interest in computers and football. I continued to see him intermittently for the remainder of the school year; then we tapered off both forms of treatment. I have kept in touch by phone with his family for the past year and, happily, his symptoms have not returned.

Mason was lucky to have parents who were so sensitive to their son; even without being able to identify a specific reason for his depression, we were eventually able to diagnose and treat it, and now his prognosis is excellent. His story highlights the importance of being alert to the symptoms of depression in your school-aged child, including the following:

- *Any of the symptoms experienced by preschoolers*
- *Frequent trips to the school nurse,* with complaints of stomachaches, headaches, nausea, or fatigue
- *Weight loss or failure to achieve expected weight gain.* Studies show that depressed kids tend to be about ten pounds lighter than children who aren't depressed. Significant weight gain can also be linked with depression in children, although this is less common.

- *Frequent verbal expressions of sadness and hopelessness,* such as "I never feel happy anymore" or "I'll never be able to do anything right."
- *Evidence of low self-esteem.* Children between the ages of six and nine are developing a sense of self; those who demonstrate poor self-esteem may well be depressed. Often, depressed kids say (or think) things like "I'm stupid" or "I like the kids in my class but they don't like me," or report that "all the other kids" call them names.
- *Frequent and excessive worrying.* All kids worry now and again. But when that worry and anxiety disrupts their lives, affecting their grades or participation in and enjoyment of various activities, it may indicate depression. For example, if a child won't play with his friend all week because he's so worried about Friday's spelling test that he spends all his time studying, there may be a problem. A child who automatically assumes that bad things will happen—the plane will crash, the picnic will be rained out, the children's museum will be closed—may be not only anxious, but also depressed.
- *Change in sleep patterns.* Some depressed children have difficulty falling asleep at bedtime; others wake in the middle of the night and can't fall back to sleep. Still other depressed kids oversleep most mornings and take an unusual number of naps during the day.
- *Excessive tearfulness* or frequently feeling that they want to cry.
- *Decreased energy or fatigue.* Depressed children often look tired, move very slowly, and have difficulty getting up in the morning. Their teachers may report that these kids fall asleep in class, and parents often feel that they have to "pump up" their children to get them to do anything.
- *Hostile or aggressive behavior.* Children aren't mean-spirted by nature; a child who seems so may actually be depressed. For instance, a youngster who constantly torments animals—unmercifully teasing the family cat or throwing sticks at the next-door neighbor's new puppy—isn't behaving normally. Other related signs of depression include excessive and unprovoked fighting with friends and classmates, and getting into frequent power struggles with Mom and Dad, like refusing to go to bed at night or to do appropriate chores.

- *Refusal or reluctance to go to school.* A one-time occurrence of such behavior is nothing to be concerned about, but a pattern can be a warning sign.

- *Drop in school performance* usually stemming from an inability to concentrate. A depressed child's grades can slip suddenly or worsen gradually over a period of several months.

- *Little interest in playing with peers.* As they go through their school-aged years, healthy children usually become increasingly involved in social activities and interactions. A child who goes in the opposite direction, who starts shying away from old friends and not making any new ones, may be depressed.

- *Poor communication skills.* Many depressed kids tend to speak in an unusually quiet, monotone voice. Often, they answer your questions with one or two words, as if their speech and language skills were underdeveloped, or the act of speaking required too much effort.

- *Repeated thoughts about or attempts to run away from home.* Such thoughts or actions generally reveal intense unhappiness or frustration, and are related to the child's desire to escape from problems that feel overwhelming.

- *Morbid or suicidal thoughts.* Kids who think about harming themselves, who have fantasies about death and dying, or who reveal repeated themes of death in their drawings or stories are often depressed. And while signs and symptoms of depression must be seen in context—that is, no single symptom necessarily indicates an emotional problem—*any* indication of suicidal thought or behavior must be taken extremely seriously. Without exception, this child needs an *immediate* professional evaluation. (For more information about suicide and children, see chapter 6.)

At a Glance: Symptoms of Depression in School-Aged Children

- Frequent and unexplained physical complaints
- Significant weight loss or gain
- Expressions of sadness or hopelessness
- Low self-esteem
- Excessive worrying
- Changes in sleep patterns
- Tearfulness
- Unprovoked hostility or aggression
- Refusal or reluctance to attend school
- Drop in grades
- Little interest in playing with others
- Poor communication
- Thoughts about or efforts to run away
- Morbid or suicidal thoughts

Depression in Adolescents

Every teenager experiences a series of challenges in life, from dealing with the physical and hormonal changes of adolescence to separating from parents and finding their own distinct identity. Teenagers' self-esteem is fragile and peer pressure intense as they strive to assume their special place in the adult world.

These challenging tasks often cause a great deal of confusion and anxiety; consequently, brief bouts of sadness—marked by tearfulness, moping, pessimism, and occasional hostility—are entirely normal during the teenage years. Often, these sad times alternate with periods of happiness, exuberance, and optimism, causing the moodiness that can make living with a teenager so trying.

But the tumultuousness of adolescence is actually an important and necessary part of growing up. It allows children to "try on" different aspects of their personality, to test the limits of their own skills and abilities—as well as the rules and expectations of family and society— and, in essence, to define themselves as unique individuals. Teenagers who don't tackle these developmental tasks successfully are at risk for depression during both adolescence and adulthood. Additionally, the normal events and transitions that occur in adolescence can trigger unresolved childhood issues which may make them more vulnerable to depression.

Here's what I mean. Kim was only four when her parents were killed in an automobile accident. She was adopted by her maternal aunt and uncle, who already had four children of their own. An easygoing and even-tempered child, Kim seemed to adjust to her new family amazingly well. As she got older, she excelled in sports, especially gymnastics. She was a good student, popular with peers and teachers alike.

When she turned sixteen, however, Kim's behavior started to change dramatically. Twice she was caught shoplifting cosmetics from a local discount store. One night, she came home drunk from a neighborhood party; although her aunt and uncle grounded her for a week, she seemed neither apologetic nor contrite. The next day, Kim told her aunt, "You know, sometimes I think this family would be better off if I wasn't around."

Two weeks later, Kim's boyfriend of six months suddenly broke up with her. Shortly thereafter, things deteriorated further. Every morning, Kim overslept and complained that she didn't want to go to school. Her grades started to slip; her last report card included a note from Kim's English teacher warning that unless her performance improved, she would not pass the course.

Kim's aunt and uncle brought their niece to a child psychiatrist for an evaluation. In the course of talking with her, the doctor learned that Kim had been having suicidal thoughts. In fact, she was hoarding pills from the family medicine cabinet and stashing them inside an old pair of hiking boots she kept at the back of her closet. Since Kim could not reassure the doctor that she would be safe at home, he decided to hospitalize her for a brief period.

While in the hospital, Kim was seen every day for individual therapy, participated in therapy groups with other adolescents, and was placed on antidepressants. After twelve days, she was no longer suicidal and returned home. (As an extra measure of protection, Kim's aunt and uncle removed all pills and other medications from the medicine cabinets.)

As Kim continued in individual therapy, her doctor began to understand that her depression centered on several factors. The normal turmoil of adolescence and the breakup with her boyfriend brought back many unresolved issues relating to the sudden death of her parents and her subsequent adoption. Within three months, however, Kim was feeling much happier and emotionally stronger. By the end of seven months, her symptoms had just about disappeared and she reported, "I feel like me again." Once treatment ended, her doctor let Kim know that she could always come by to talk with him if she began to feel a bit shaky again.

As Kim's story shows, the signs of teenage depression are multiple and varied. Many are similar to the symptoms seen in school-aged kids, including a drop in grades, expressions of sadness or hopelessness, poor self-esteem, fatigue or lethargy, difficulty sleeping or oversleeping, apathy toward or sudden dislike of activities they used to enjoy, and, of course, morbid or suicidal thoughts or actions. But there are additional symptoms, including the following:

- *Difficulty in maintaining relationships.* Depressed teens may start to cut themselves off from others, breaking up with boy- or girlfriends, rejecting friendships, and refusing to participate in school events.
- *Self-destructive behaviors.* Teenagers who drink and then drive, have promiscuous, unsafe sex, abuse drugs, or harm their bodies (for instance, excessively picking at pimples or biting their fingernails to the point of bleeding) despite understanding the hazards to their health and safety are often showing signs of depression.
- *Eating-related difficulties,* including a sudden loss of appetite, bingeing and purging, or drastically reducing food intake. While these behaviors may be signs of depression, they are also symptoms of serious eating disorders, such as bulimia nervosa (characterized by bingeing and purging), and anorexia nervosa (marked by excessive weight loss and a distorted body image). Clinical experience with teenagers, particularly girls, reveals that depression may underlie or even trigger an

eating disorder, or the two may coexist as separate problems. In either case, teens with eating-related problems should be seen by a qualified professional. (See chapter 4 for more on the link between eating disorders and depression.)

- *Antisocial or even delinquent behavior.* This sign includes a broad range of behaviors, from lying to parents or friends, to cheating on school exams, to shoplifting and drinking while driving.
- *Social isolation.* Depressed teens often become isolated from friends and family, spending long periods of time alone. They may refuse to join family outings and projects, preferring instead to be left by themselves.
- *Frequently feeling that nobody understands them.* Depressed teens often feel that they are different from everybody else and disapproved of by family, friends, and teachers.
- *Restlessness, grouchiness, sulkiness, excessive moodiness.*
- *Unintentional weight loss or gain.*
- *Problems at school.* The symptoms include a drop in grades, difficulty getting along with teachers or peers, or a reluctance to go to school.
- *Inattention to personal appearance.* Parents may not always like or understand the way their teenagers look, balking at their choice of clothes, pierced bodies, or extreme hairstyles. But children who intentionally look a certain way because that's what's "in" are behaving perfectly appropriately; they're kids trying to create an identity that's separate from yours. On the other hand, children who are sloppy because they have low self-esteem and truly don't care about how they look could well be depressed.
- *Extreme sensitivity to rejection or failure.* Everyone gets upset when they're rejected or fail at something they try. But most people get over it pretty quickly. Depressed teenagers, however, allow rejection or failure to disrupt their functioning. When their boy- or girlfriend breaks up with them, when they fail to get the summer job they had their heart set on, or when they get a C in French instead of the B they were striving for, they become distraught, tearful, withdrawn, or can't eat or sleep well for weeks on end.
- *Reduced physical activity.* Normal teenagers are usually full of energy

and vigor. Depressed teens tend to suffer from lethargy and often seem to drag themselves around.

- *Restlessness or fidgeting.* Younger children are often fidgety and restless; they cannot be expected to sit still for long periods of time. But teenagers should have a great deal more control over their bodies; when they don't, it can be a sign of clinical depression.
- *Morbid or suicidal thoughts or actions.* Focusing on death-related themes in their choice of games, music, art, or reading matter can be a sign of depression in adolescents. Suicidal thoughts or comments should always be taken very seriously and require immediate attention and evaluation. (For more on children and suicide, see chapter 6.)

At a Glance: Symptoms of Depression in Adolescents

- Drop in school grades and/or conduct
- Behavior problems in school
- Feelings of sadness or hopelessness
- Low self-esteem
- Fatigue
- Changes in sleep patterns
- Loss of enjoyment of previously enjoyable activities
- Self-destructive behavior
- Difficulty with relationships
- Eating-related problems
- Antisocial or delinquent behavior
- Social isolation
- Inattention to appearance
- Extreme sensitivity to rejection or failure
- Physical slowness or agitation
- Morbid or suicidal thoughts or actions

As a concerned, sensitive parent, it's easy to become overly vigilant in looking for the signs and symptoms of depression in your child. But try to strike a balance: While you want to be alert to any changes in your child's behavior, you also don't want to jump to conclusions. Remember that in and of itself, no individual behavior *necessarily* signals depression in your child or—with the exception of suicidal thoughts, statements, or actions—demands immediate attention. Instead, it is the constellation of depressive signs and symptoms, combined with your own parental instincts, that will let you know when it's time to seek professional help. If you have persistent questions or doubts, however, it's always best to err on the side of safety and caution, and have your child evaluated by a trained mental health clinician.

Chapter

4

Depression's Link with Other Problems

When I'm depressed I feel sad, but it's a different kind of sad—not like when I can't go outside or I don't get something I want. That goes away. This sad stays a really long time. It goes all the way to my bones.

—Mark, age nine

Eight-year-old Matthew couldn't stop fidgeting in class. He was always dropping his pencils and papers, then scrambling out of his seat to retrieve them. Several times a day he would jump up and run out of the classroom to get a drink of water or shout out answers to questions though the teacher hadn't called on him. Although he was bright, Matthew didn't do well in school. His teacher felt his inability to pay attention prevented him from working up to his potential.

Matthew's teacher suspected Attention Deficit Hyperactivity Disorder (ADHD), which she knew was characterized by impulsivity and difficulty sitting still. She spoke to Matthew's parents about it, recommending that they ask their pediatrician to give him some medication to calm him down.

Matthew's doctor found the youngster in good physical health. A series of routine blood tests also proved normal. Although she was not sure whether he had ADHD, she prescribed Ritalin, a drug commonly used to treat ADHD, to see if it would help his behavior.

After two weeks, Matthew seemed a bit calmer, but he was still disruptive in class, and his attention span and ability to concentrate had not really improved. One afternoon at recess, he bloodied the nose of a classmate in a fight and was sent to see the guidance counselor. When she asked Matthew why he had punched his friend, Matthew shrugged his shoulders and said, "I don't *know* why. It's like I'm just mad all the time."

That's when Matthew's parents brought their son to see me. In an early session, when Matthew and I were playing games and drawing, he said he wanted to draw me a picture. He picked up a black crayon and began scribbling furiously all over the page. Then, in the one remaining empty corner, he drew two big black ovals. When I asked him to tell me about his drawing, he said, "This is my life. And these (pointing to the ovals) are tears."

As we worked together, it became clear that Matthew was a very sad, depressed little boy who was filled with self-doubt. He felt he wasn't as good as the other kids, that he was "geeky and weird." He also told me that he had trouble falling asleep at night, and that he often woke up in the morning feeling "like something bad is going to happen."

I understood why Matthew's teacher and pediatrician suspected ADHD; he did have a number of characteristic symptoms. But after completing my clinical evaluation, I felt that his underlying problem was depression. I shared my ideas with Matthew's parents. Together, we agreed on a course of treatment that included my working individually with the youngster and changing his medication from Ritalin to an antidepressant. I also recommended that his parents see a social worker skilled at helping moms and dads cope with kids' challenging behaviors.

Within a few weeks, Matthew began to show significant improvement; he calmed down in class, began sleeping better, and found it easier to concentrate. Four months later, his symptoms had all but disappeared. When I asked Matthew what had changed for him he said, "Well, it's like I'm not so mad. I don't feel like I have to fight with everyone anymore. My shoulders don't seem so heavy."

When It's Not Just Depression

Matthew's story isn't all that unusual. Depression is misdiagnosed—or simply missed—in many children. And not without reason.

As we discussed earlier, depression has a wide range of symptoms, from "feeling sad" to "feeling mad," from withdrawing from others to lashing out at them. What's more, how depression looks in a particular child depends on the youngster's temperament, personality, age, and developmental level. A teenager who "acts out" her depression is more likely to shoplift, cut school, engage in promiscuous sex, or mix drinking and driving; a younger depressed child, on the other hand, might throw repeated temper tantrums, frequently whine and cry, or stubbornly refuse to follow household rules.

But there's another factor that makes it hard to recognize depression in a child: its close link with other emotional problems.

Several years ago, I was working on an inpatient child psychiatry unit at a Boston hospital when we got a call from a researcher who wanted to do a study comparing children with ADHD, conduct disorder, and depression. We thought about it but turned him down. The reason: Almost every child on our unit had symptoms consistent with all three diagnoses.

But that's not unusual. Many symptoms of depression, including overactivity and restlessness, irritability, a low tolerance for frustration, and hostile or aggressive behavior (like biting or kicking), are shared by a number of other conditions, including those the researcher wanted to study. Further, an individual child may have more than one problem. For example, a youngster can suffer from ADHD *and* depression at the same time, or have an eating disorder *along with* depression. In fact, certain problems—like a severe learning disability or conduct disorder—can actually put your child at greater risk for depression, as I will explain shortly. Treating him for one problem and ignoring the other won't help that child overcome his difficulties and become a healthy and happy adult.

To complicate matters more, the symptoms of depression may be obscured by other emotional disorders. This is often the case with drug or alcohol abuse. For instance, a colleague of mine recently treated a sixteen-year-old boy for alcohol abuse. But once the child achieved control over his drinking and was able to keep away from alcohol for several months, the signs of his underlying clinical depression began to emerge. The fact was that his problem was exacerbated by depression; he often used alcohol to dull his emotional pain.

Since many books have been written about the individual ailments that most often overlap, coexist, or underlie depression, it's not necessary—or appropriate—for me to go into these disorders in great depth here. But I do think it's helpful to explore them briefly, focusing our attention on their special links with clinical depression.

Attention Deficit Hyperactivity Disorder

The popularity of several recent books on ADHD, particularly *Driven to Distraction,* by my colleagues Edward Hallowell, M.D., and John Ratey, M.D., have helped focus a great deal of attention on this disorder. (See "Additional Reading—for Parents" at the end of this book.) In one way, that's wonderful, because it means that more kids who need help for ADHD will get it. In another way, however, it's disturbing, because in many cases, children who show *any* symptoms of ADHD—like being disruptive in class or fidgeting and being extremely restless—are being put on medication (usually, but not always, Ritalin) *before* a formal diagnosis is made by a qualified mental health professional. Too often, these children either don't really have ADHD or have ADHD *and* another disorder, like depression, which is going untreated. (In any case, medication alone is almost never the best way to treat a child's emotional disorder. Instead, children need a comprehensive treatment approach that usually includes individual therapy as well as work with the family and the school—but more on this in chapter 8.)

To help ensure that your child does not pay the high price of an incorrect or incomplete diagnosis, you need to become more familiar with ADHD. Here's some information that should help.

Attention Deficit Hyperactivity Disorder is thought to be caused by a neurochemical problem that makes it difficult for a child to pay attention, focus on a task, or control his impulses. Most ADHD develops in children under age seven and is marked by symptomatic behaviors that continue for at least six months.

The typical symptoms of ADHD are:

- excessive fidgeting of the hands or feet
- difficulty sitting still or staying seated
- jumping from one uncompleted task to another
- continally interrupting other people's conversations, or disrupting other children's games
- appearing not to pay attention to what is being said
- engaging in dangerous activities without thinking about the consequences

If you think back to our discussion of the symptoms of depression in chapter 3, you'll notice a fair amount of overlap between ADHD and depression. In fact, many depressed children—and children who have ADHD—go through times when they suffer from many of the same symptoms, including excessive crying or sadness; self-destructive acts; intense worrying; irritability and temper tantrums; restlessness and overactivity, or social withdrawal; and difficulty concentrating. So before you accept any diagnosis of ADHD—particularly if you suspect that your child may be depressed or is at risk for depression—make sure that she has a comprehensive evaluation that includes a physical exam performed by a medical doctor, as well as assessments for emotional, academic, and social abilities. And if you have any doubts about the validity of the diagnosis, get a second opinion.

Conduct Disorder

Conduct disorder is a behavioral and emotional problem that afflicts many youngsters. Kids with conduct disorder typically and consistently violate the rights of others or the rules of society in a way that is not appropriate for their age. For example, a twenty-two-month-old who pushes a playmate down and yanks her toy away is acting pretty normally; a ten-year-old who frequently does the same thing is not and may be suffering from an emotional problem like conduct disorder.

Among symptoms most commonly associated with conduct disorder are:

- bullying others
- initiating fights
- being physically cruel to people and/or animals
- using any kind of weapon, such as a bat, pipe, or knife, to hurt others
- being consistently disobedient
- stealing
- lying to or "conning" others
- intentionally destroying others' property, for example deliberately setting fires
- repeatedly attempting to run away from home
- truancy

If you compare these symptoms with those of depression, you will see that, again, many are the same. In some cases, the child with conduct disorder may also have an underlying or coexisting depression. For example, a 1987 study of depressed children conducted by Javad Kashani, M.D., a psychiatrist who has done a great deal of research in depression, found conduct disorder in 33 percent of the depressed kids.

In earlier work with depressed boys who had not yet gone through puberty, renowned researcher Joachim Puig-Antich, M.D., found that 37 percent of the youngsters also met the diagnostic criteria for conduct disorder. Further study revealed that in 87 percent of the cases, the depression appeared prior to the conduct disorder. Significantly, when the children in the study were treated with antidepressant medication, the symptoms of conduct disorder—*and* of depression—were almost completely eliminated.

Whenever I think about the link between conduct disorder and depression, I remember nine-year-old Justin. He was referred to me by a school psychologist who believed the child had conduct disorder. His impression was understandable; apparently, Justin repeatedly had stolen lunch money from his classmates, often skipped school, and had set several fires in the school playground. These problems had been escalating throughout the school year.

But after working with Justin and speaking with his father, I doubted that conduct disorder was the right diagnosis. I learned that last year, his younger brother, Sean, had been diagnosed with leukemia, and that his mother and Sean recently had left for a long-term stay at a cancer center in the Midwest. Justin was left in the care of an aunt he barely knew and a father who worked long, late hours. Understandably, Justin was extremely upset and depressed by these changes in his life and, I felt certain, was acting out his upset through the hostile behaviors that had been too quickly labeled as conduct disorder. I believed that depression was at the root of his problem and shared my convictions with his father and aunt.

I began treating Justin for depression, working with him weekly in one-on-one psychotherapy sessions. After about six weeks, Justin felt safe enough in therapy to express his upset and confusion and to use role-playing games, action figures, and drawings to tell his story. (Because I was concerned about his fire setting, I also referred him to a special fire-safety program offered through a local children's psychiatric clinic.) Soon, his depression began to lift; his school attendance improved and he began to make new friends. Over time, just about all the symptoms that had led to the initial assumption of conduct disorder virtually disappeared.

Anxiety Disorders

Occasional anxiety is normal for children of all ages. Healthy babies, toddlers, and even preschoolers become anxious when separated from their parents or caregivers. Older children experience anxiety over such stressful events as an upcoming exam, a team tryout, or first date. But when a child's anxieties become so severe that they stop her from participating in daily activities—going to school, attending a friend's birthday party, playing with the other kids on the block—she may be suffering from an anxiety disorder.

Among the telltale symptoms of an anxiety disorder are:

- constant worrying about the future, particularly about your own or a loved one's safety
- restlessness
- frequent nightmares
- trouble thinking clearly
- reluctance or refusal to go to school
- unexplained stomachaches, headaches, or other aches and pains
- extreme thoughts or fears about sleeping away from home, and/or panic attacks or tantrums when separated from parents or familiar surroundings
- overly clingy or needy behavior
- withdrawn behavior, and overall tension and uneasiness

Anxiety and depression frequently coexist in such a way as to make it hard to tell which is the core problem. A youngster who is depressed may become anxious over her increasing inability to cope with life's everyday struggles. Conversely, an extremely anxious child who has difficulty coping with everyday stresses and strains may start feeling bad about herself—and this drop in self-esteem can lead to depression. In fact, in two 1988 studies—one with young children and the other with teenagers—as many as three-quarters of depressed adolescents and a third of clinically depressed younger children also suffered from anxiety disorder.

One of the major forms of anxiety problems affecting children is *obsessive-compulsive disorder* (OCD). Children with OCD have recurrent, unwanted, and unpleasant thoughts. They worry excessively about things like dirt, germs, and contamination. They demand extreme order and symmetry, and can't throw out any possessions, no matter how useless or worn out. Compulsions range from excessive washing (especially hand washing, bathing, and toothbrushing) to repetitive and almost ritualistic behaviors, like continuously going in and out of doors, getting up and sitting down, repeating phrases, checking to make sure windows and doors are locked or that homework is done "right," as well as touching, counting, and rearranging objects around them. Children with OCD often suffer from depression and develop many of its symptoms.

While no one knows exactly what causes OCD, researchers strongly suspect that, like depression, it involves an imbalance of the chemicals of the brain. OCD most frequently strikes adolescents and young adults, although children as young as five have been diagnosed with the disorder. Research shows that when children under thirteen are affected, boys outnumber girls by a ratio of at least two to one.

While OCD sufferers are usually aware of their irrational behaviors and fears, they are powerless to control them without professional treatment. But because victims fear their friends and family will think they're crazy, they often go to great lengths to keep their symptoms secret, which makes diagnosis—and proper treatment—extremely difficult.

However, the following hard-to-hide symptoms could tip you off to the onset of OCD in your child:

- erasing so often that the paper begins to tear
- repeatedly retracing letters or words; continually rereading the same paragraph(s)
- refusing to use a towel more than once until it is laundered
- repeatedly stopping up the toilet because a fear of germs makes them use too much paper
- rigid bedtime rituals
- asking to have phrases repeated over and over again
- constantly worrying that they may be getting sick

It's important to seek help if your child has any of these symptoms. He may be suffering from an anxiety disorder, an underlying depression, or both. Having your youngster thoroughly evaluated and treated by a qualified mental health professional is the best step to take.

Eating Disorders

Overeating and undereating are pretty common problems for children. Kids often eat too much or too little when they're anxious and tense, when they're following the latest fad diet, or when they've developed poor nutritional habits. But children who are *completely* preoccupied with food—either persistently bingeing or refusing to eat—may well have a true eating disorder.

Believe it or not, an estimated 43 percent of individuals with eating disorders report that their problem started before the age of sixteen; 10 percent of those people said their disorder began before age eleven. Eating disorders have even been reported in children as young as five!

The two most common eating disorders affecting children are *anorexia nervosa,* a condition in which the child denies herself food because of an irrational fear of becoming fat, and *bulimia nervosa,* binge eating that's frequently followed by purging in some way (vomiting or using laxatives or diuretics).

Eating disorders should not be taken lightly. They are very serious illnesses that can lead to dehydration, hormonal imbalances, heart problems, damage to other vital organs, and, in some cases, death. Unfortunately, eating disorders are hard for parents and caregivers to spot, because children are often quite adept at hiding their symptoms. Kids who suffer from bulimia, for example, often eat large amounts of food at the dinner table—so Mom and Dad think everything's fine—then excuse themselves and go to the bathroom to purge, running water in the sink or tub to cover the sound of their vomiting.

But if you stay on your toes, you may be able to spot some of the most common symptoms. For anorexia nervosa, these include:

- abnormal weight loss
- persistent, intense fear of gaining weight or "getting fat"
- refusal to eat all but the tiniest portions of food
- compulsive exercising
- distorted body image
- unusual sensitivity to cold

- no menstrual period, or irregular periods
- hair loss

For bulimia nervosa, common symptoms are:

- preoccupation with food
- secret binge eating
- purging after eating
- abuse of laxatives, diuretics, diet pills, and emetics
- compulsive exercising
- swollen salivary glands
- broken blood vessels in eyes

Among all children, teenage girls are most at risk for eating disorders. Interestingly, youngsters with these disorders are often perfectionistic and tend to do well at school; they frequently get high grades and actively participate in many extracurricular events. But it's important not to be fooled by this high-achieving behavior. Often, it masks a poor sense of self-esteem and a negative or distorted body image. It's not hard, then, to understand why eating disorders and clinical depression often coexist—and why treating one and ignoring the other won't work. To give your child the best chance for success, both disorders need to be diagnosed accurately and treated by a trained professional.

Learning Disabilities

The link between learning disabilities and depression is strong. These disorders share many symptoms, such as a decline in school grades, a short attention span, difficulty paying attention in class, and a lack of interest in school. What's more, learning disabilities can lead to depression.

Here's why. When a learning disability isn't accurately detected and treated, it often has a "snowball" effect. For example, children whose learning problem makes it difficult to master grammar in elementary school also have problems writing essays and compositions in later grades. Try as they might, they seem unable to develop these skills and become increasingly frustrated by their repeated failures. Sometimes, these children with learning disabilities misbehave in class because they'd rather be labeled "bad" than "dumb." After a while, these repeated negative experiences lead to emotional problems and, often, depression.

This does not have to happen, however. Learning disabilities are highly treatable. But first, they need to be identified—and that's where you come in. Spotting the earliest signs of a learning disability and getting your child the help he needs can keep a learning problem from developing into a serious emotional disorder. So be sure to seek a professional evaluation if your child shows any of the following:

- an attention span that seems especially short, particularly when compared to other children of the same age
- difficulty understanding and following instructions
- problems mastering reading, writing, or math skills
- reversing letters or numbers, such as confusing *62* with *26*, or *b* with *d* or *no* with *on*
- coordination problems in sports or in such small-motor tasks as holding a pencil or tying a shoelace
- school grades that seem far below the child's abilities
- constantly misplacing belongings
- overactivity or restlessness

Once your child's learning disability has been identified, treatment will most likely involve several measures. Your child may need to attend special-educational classes and, in severe cases, to go to a special school. And in most cases, both parents and teachers will need to work with the child to build (or, in many cases, rebuild) his confidence and strengthen his self-esteem.

Substance Abuse

One of the saddest realities of today's world is the enormous number of children who abuse drugs and/or alcohol. According to recent statistics released from the National Institute on Drug Abuse, two-thirds of eighth graders say they've already tried alcohol, and 25 percent say they are current drinkers. Marijuana use among children this age more than doubled between 1991 and 1994, from slightly over 6 percent to fully 13 percent. The average age when a child first tries alcohol is eleven; for marijuana, it's twelve!

A report issued by the U.S. Department of Health and Human Services posits the reason for all this bad news. Apparently, the antidrug attitude that gained momentum in the late 1980s has lost steam. Today, a declining number of children ages twelve to seventeen believe that illegal drugs are harmful to their health. While in general, females still lag behind males in substance abuse, a study conducted by the National Center on Addiction and Substance Abuse at Columbia University found that this gender gap has narrowed among young people. In fact, now about as many teenage girls drink as do adolescent boys. Another disturbing statistic: Teenage girls are more than fifteen times more likely to have started using illegal substances by age fifteen than their mothers.

Sadly, there's a powerful link between substance abuse and depression. Depression is a common symptom of substance abuse because kids who take illicit drugs or drink alcohol often become depressed. Additionally, many kids who abuse drugs or alcohol, particularly those who do it regularly, are *already* depressed and trying to soothe or escape their painful feelings with drugs and/or alcohol.

Once again, early recognition and treatment is the best way to help children overcome the physical and emotional problems associated with substance abuse. Here are some of the most common warning signs:

- repeated physical problems, including fatigue, red and dull eyes, excessive sniffling, red and runny nose, or steady cough
- sudden and severe mood swings

- an abrupt change in personality
- poor self-esteem
- depression and its symptoms, including sad mood, withdrawal, and social isolation
- argumentativeness
- breaking family and school rules, or breaking the law
- declining grades
- cutting classes or skipping school altogether
- associating with new friends who are uninterested in activities the child previously enjoyed
- intentional disregard for appearance

If you suspect your child is abusing drugs or alcohol, talk with her about it. I know that it's a hard conversation to have and that you can expect to encounter lots of denial, like "I don't know how that stuff got in my drawer," or "It isn't mine; I was just holding it for a friend," or "Someone must have put that beer in my locker just to get me in trouble; I never saw it before." But don't accept these excuses; it won't help you or your child. Instead, seek professional guidance—speak with your child's pediatrician, or ask advice of someone specially trained in childhood substance abuse at a local treatment center. Remember: A youngster who is abusing drugs or alcohol needs special help both for this problem and, if necessary, for the underlying or coexisting depression or other emotional difficulty.

What You Can Do

It's not your job to *diagnose* depression or any other emotional disorder in your child. But it is your job to *try to recognize* a problem and get your child the help she needs as early as possible, when treatment is most effective. It's also your responsibility to take emotional diagnoses seriously. In fact, I urge you *not* to accept any diagnosis without doing the following:

- *Have your child evaluated by a qualified professional* whom you trust. He should be well trained and experienced in dealing with children with depression and other emotional disorders. And he should spend enough time with your child to do a comprehensive evaluation; it's impossible to gather all the information necessary to fully evaluate a child in a single, twenty-minute session. (For more on how to find the right professional for your child, see chapter 7.)

- *Provide the professional with any information* that could help him understand your child and reach an accurate diagnosis. For example, be sure to report any sudden changes in your child's life, including a move to a new neighborhood, a change of schools, your separation or divorce, or any losses the child has experienced recently, such as the death of a family member or pet.

- *Ask lots of questions* of the clinician making the diagnosis. Inquire how he arrived at that diagnosis, whether he considered other possible disorders (such as depression) *and* why he ruled them out. You should also understand the course of treatment he is recommending, its risks, and how you can help monitor any possible side effects or observe progress; in other words, you want to know how your child's behavior could or should change. (For more on the most helpful questions to ask your child's doctor, see chapter 7.)

- *Listen to your instincts.* No one knows your child better than you do. If you any have doubts about your doctor's recommendations, get a second opinion. No reputable mental health professional will discourage you from getting additional expert advice; in fact, he'll probably make it easier for you by giving you referrals and be sharing information and ideas with any other professional you consult.

Of course, many children with ADHD, conduct or anxiety disorder, or any other illness we've just discussed *do not* have depression, either as a coexisting or underlying problem. But many do. And when that depression is overlooked and ignored, the children are more likely to suffer negative consequences for many years to come.

So advocate for proper and early diagnosis. You'll be giving your kids the best opportunity for future health and happiness.

Chapter

5

Everybody's Crisis:

Depression's Impact on You

and Your Family

Last year, I found out that my father got married without telling me. He just picked me up one day and told me. I felt sad and angry. I got so mad I wanted to set his house on fire. That made my mother sad, and my little brother got scared. Then I felt even sadder.

—Sam, age eight

When a child suffers from depression, the problem reverberates throughout the entire family, catching everyone up in the emotional turmoil it brings. Parents are especially hard hit since they must learn not only to cope with the depressed child's provocative behavior, but also to respond patiently and lovingly to that child, keep him from harming himself and others, and encourage him to behave in a way that will help him get along in the world. At the same time, parents need to attend to the needs of the other members of their family and, if Mom and Dad work outside the home, to the demands of their employer, co-workers, and clients.

Dealing with so many pressures and different agendas is a lot for anyone to handle, so it's only natural that as a parent of a depressed child, you sometimes feel stretched too thin. But don't despair. Often, simply understanding how a depressed child can affect you and your family makes the enormous strain feel much more manageable.

<u>Two Ways to Look at It</u>

In this chapter, we'll look at two different but equally significant issues: first, how the family affects the child—that is, the kinds of family dynamics that often surround childhood depression—and second, how the child affects the family. Then, we'll take a separate look at the impact a youngster's depression has on individual family members as well as on various types of families, including traditional, two parent, single parent, and stepfamilies. Finally, we'll explore some of the most effective ways to help you and your family cope.

<u>Distinct Family Patterns</u>

Parents don't cause depression; neither do other relatives. But as I've said earlier, sometimes family dynamics clearly contribute to the development of depression in a child. Here are some of the most common and troublesome patterns.

- **Families with Physical or Emotional Abuse**
 Depression often develops in homes in which children are physically or emotionally abused. And that's a lot of homes. Well over three million youngsters were reported abused or neglected in this country in 1995 alone, according to the National Committee to Prevent Child Abuse. And in a national survey conducted by researchers at the Family Research Laboratory at the University of New Hampshire, fully 25 percent of children ages ten through sixteen said they've been assaulted or abused in the previous year.
 The abuse may not have *caused* the depression; as we've already discussed, your child's neurobiological makeup or strong family history

of depression may have predisposed her toward the problem. But without question, an abusive home environment can make matters worse.

Children who grow up in abusive families tend to develop a distorted image of themselves as bad and unlovable. It's not hard to understand why. If you're a little kid and your mom or dad abuses you, it's scary to believe that your parent is doing something bad. So the solution is to convince yourself that it's your fault. Not only are abused children failing to get their emotional—and sometimes physical—needs met, but they are collecting a catalog of negative and stressful life experiences which, as we saw in chapter 2, increases their risk for depression.

■ Families with Substance Abuse Problems

Children who grow up in homes marked by drug or alcohol abuse develop problems similar to those of kids raised in abusive families. If a child's mother or father is drinking, the thought that "my parent is out of control" is very frightening because it means that the child must admit that Mom or Dad can't take care of him. So instead, the child believes, "I did something bad and that's why Mommy (or Daddy) is drinking." These kinds of thoughts, replayed over and over, make the child feel bad about himself which, in turn, increases the likelihood of depression.

Children raised by a mother or father who abuses drugs or alcohol can also suffer from unpredictable, inconsistent parenting. The lack of a stable and secure home base makes it difficult for these children to feel safe enough to explore the world around them and to enjoy simple, pleasurable experiences—like having friends over without worrying that their mom or dad will be drunk or stoned—that will help them to become confident, resilient individuals who can defend themselves against depression.

These children can also get extremely angry at their parent for the addictive (or abusive) behavior. But once again, this powerful emotion can be frightening. So instead of directing their anger at their mom or dad, they often turn their anger inward against themselves and develop depression.

■ Families Who Criticize Too Much

Suppose a child becomes very listless, continually complaining that he's "too tired" to do his homework or to complete his chores. Rather than talking to the child to find out what's wrong, some parents become so angry and frustrated that they overreact and get verbally abusive, saying things like "Why are you so lazy?" "Can't you do anything right?" "You better shape up fast, young man, or you can forget about playing soccer this season!" Over time, the child begins to believe that he *is* lazy and can't do anything right. He develops a negative self-image that makes him more vulnerable to depression.

■ Idealizing Families

In other families, children are treated in a different but also inappropriate way. These kids are put on a pedestal; every feeling and minor achievement is considered momentous. The child is an "angel" above reproach. If her grades slip, it's the fault of the teacher, the school system, the influence of classmates, television, and so forth. Because idealized children never learn to accept responsibility for their actions, they often grow up with an unrealistic view of themselves. When they move beyond their family and into new, more judgmental environments like school—where teachers, coaches, and classmates treat them more realistically—these children, who have such an artificially inflated but fragile sense of self-esteem, may overreact to failure, rejection, or minor disappointments, which increases their risk for depression.

■ Families Who Don't React Enough

In other families children's words and actions don't seem to matter. When the child becomes upset—because he gets an unexpectedly poor grade or doesn't get invited to a classmate's party—he receives neither support nor sympathy from his family. In fact, he doesn't get much reaction at all. This lack of attention and acknowledgement conveys the message that the events of his life are inconsequential and that he himself is not important.

■ Families Already Coping with Depression

As we discussed in chapter 2, children who grow up in families already coping with depression—especially a depressed parent—often learn that depression is an appropriate and acceptable response to stress. When these children confront an obstacle or experience a setback, like failing to make the starting team, they are more likely to become depressed themselves. These children don't just mimic the behavior of their depressed parent or sibling; clinical experience shows that they actually become depressed. To these kids, "being like Mom" or "being like Dad" means being depressed.

Sometimes, when children realize that their depressed relative is the center of attention, they become depressed in an attempt to get more attention and nurturance for themselves. They don't do this on purpose, of course; in most cases, they are totally unaware of the factors influencing their behavior.

Further, children living in families in which a parent or sibling suffers from clinical depression often blame themselves for their loved one's illness. These negative feelings can and often do lead to the development of their own depression.

Consider the story of Sara and her daughter. Years ago, I worked as a psychiatrist in a hospital emergency room. My job was to evaluate whether suicidal patients should go back home, remain in the hospital, or be admitted to another treatment program. One night, Sara, age thirty-six, was brought in to the emergency room. She had tried to kill herself by taking an overdose of over-the-counter headache medication. It took several hours for the ER staff to stabilize her medically, after which I was called in to evaluate her emotional condition. After an extensive interview, I concluded she was no longer acutely suicidal. I also learned that she was already in treatment with a psychiatrist and, with Sara's permission, spoke with him by phone. Sara agreed to see him first thing in the morning and her sister, who had accompanied her to the hospital, assured me that she would stay overnight with Sara and make certain that she kept her appointment.

But there was one more problem that concerned me: Sara had a seven-year-old daughter at home. Apparently, she'd been the one who found Sara asleep on the living room sofa; when she couldn't wake her up, she'd called 911. Since I knew that children with a depressed parent are at high risk for depression themselves—and that this child was likely to have trouble dealing with her mom's crisis—I encouraged Sara to bring her daughter to see me. In working with the child, I quickly realized that she had linked a number of unrelated incidents to the suicide attempt. Specifically, the youngster, who had brought home a disciplinary note from her teacher and threw a temper tantrum in the supermarket, believed that these events had caused her mother's suicide attempt. Tearfully, the child said to me, "I promise to be good so that Mommy won't get mad or sad anymore." Clearly, this youngster was at high risk for depression at least in part because of her mom's emotional problems and suicide attempt.

■ Families with Difficulties Expressing Emotions

Families have different emotional styles and ways of expressing feelings. Highly emotional families express every feeling and talk about every issue that arises, no matter how small and inconsequential. Emotionally closed families keep all their feelings under wraps, refusing to discuss even major crises, like a death in the family, or a parent's alcoholic rages. In other families, relatives are free to express certain emotions, such as anger, but must suppress others, like sadness or grief.

Families with such skewed patterns of emotional expression increase children's risk of depression by failing to provide emotional perspective and appropriate, necessary outlets for their feelings. Children who are raised in overly emotional families, for example, may grow up believing that every problem or disappointment, no matter how small, is a crisis. Kids who grow up in families in which emotions are denied or dismissed learn that expressing their feelings isn't important or permissable. In either case, these children are at risk for depression because they fail to learn healthy ways of expressing their feelings and to develop a balanced emotional perspective.

■ Families Without Consistent Structure or Limits

Some families don't function in any sort of predictable, structured manner. Bedtimes and mealtimes are random, rules are not enforced consistently, and family rituals like holiday gatherings or birthday parties are not regularly celebrated.

Now, I'm not suggesting that families should be run like military troops. Real life doesn't work that way. When Mom or Dad gets stuck in traffic, dinner may be late; when a special program is on TV, bedtime may get pushed back an hour. But in families where there is *never* any structure and where unpredictability prevails, two problems can arise. First, children grow accustomed to chaotic environments. When they find themselves in more organized, formal settings, like school, they have difficulty coping, often getting into trouble with teachers and classmates. If such negative interactions occur repeatedly, over time the child can develop a poor self-image and become more vulnerable to depression.

Second, when children grow up in families that don't offer reliability and predictability, they often feel insecure and unsafe, and are more likely to develop depression.

How It Works in Real Life: One Family's Story

While categorizing families helps us understand how depression is connected to certain family dynamics, in real life there tends to be a lot of overlap. That is, one family may overreact to the children's feelings *and* fail to set limits *and* provide an unpredictable environment.

The story of the J.s offers a telling example. At age fourteen, Susan J. was referred to an outpatient crisis center after wielding a pocket knife and threatening to kill herself. In the course of her treatment, which included intensive family therapy, I also met her mom, dad, and ten-year-old brother, Trevor.

The family dynamics were very revealing. Dad, forty-two, who described his own parents as "kind of closed off and unable to show their feelings," was himself a brooding, emotionally distant father. Mom was an anxious, introverted woman of thirty-five. When Dad got laid off from his job as an electrical contractor—a situation that scared and infuriated him—he took his anger out on his wife and was verbally abusive toward her. Mom, fearful of standing up to her husband, took her resentment out on her children, constantly yelling at and berating them.

Both parents saw Trevor as the "real problem child." And indeed, during counseling sessions, he constantly engaged in provocative behaviors, throwing toys around the room, banging his fists against the wall, throwing a woolen cap at his sister's head. His parents seemed unable to set any limits for Trevor, alternately laughing at his actions and warning him to stop.

After a few sessions, I realized that both children were depressed. Susan expressed her sadness by moping around the house, withdrawing from friends, and, ultimately, threatening suicide. She believed that her parents were so focused on her brother's antics that they never had any time for her. "It's like I'm invisible, like nobody cares," Susan said. "It's always Trevor. The only time my parents paid any attention was when they thought I was going to hurt myself."

Trevor's depression presented itself in a different way. While Susan "acted in," Trevor "acted out," disobeying his parents, teasing his sister, and picking fights with other kids at school. His drawings, too, were revealing. When asked to sketch a picture of his family, he drew his mother on one side, his father on the other, and himself and his sister squarely in the middle; everyone was shouting at one another.

While I continued to work with the whole family, I also arranged for Susan and Trevor to see individual therapists in my group practice, and I referred the parents for couples counseling. After two months, both children are doing significantly better. The parents are making a greater effort to work out their anger with each other, and their fighting and screaming has calmed considerably. They are also trying to spend more time together enjoying things as a family.

Susan and Trevor are learning how to express their feelings more openly and how to vent their anger, hurt, and frustration in less destructive ways. A telling picture Trevor drew several weeks into therapy still showed his parents fighting, but now he and his sister were off to one side riding their bikes together. The intensity of Trevor's anger has decreased, and he no longer sees himself and his sister in the middle of their parents' arguments—certainly a step in the right direction.

How a Child's Depression Affects Other Family Members

We've spent the first part of this chapter learning how certain family dynamics can contribute to the development of childhood depression. But a clinically depressed child also has a dramatic effect on the dynamics of the family. Mothers, fathers, sisters, and brothers often experience a wide range of powerful emotions, from sorrow and anxiety to resentment and anger to compassion and hope. Family members can become emotionally and physically exhausted as they try to deal with the recurring demands and crises of the depressed child. Some families are drawn closer together by a child's depression, lending one another enormous emotional and practical support; others break apart under the strain. To understand this more fully, let's take a closer look at how a depressed child can affect the rest of the family.

▪ How a Child's Depression Affects Parents

Learning that your child is depressed and trying to get him the help he needs place extraordinary emotional demands on parents. Parents often go through several stages: shock, followed by denial; they hope that their child is going through a difficult stage that will pass, or is suffering from a simple physical ailment that, once treated, will make him "normal" again.

Next, many parents feel anger and disappointment. They say, "This is not what I expected when I had this child. Why can't he just shape up and act right?" Then comes recognition, often followed by genuine grief as they watch the child they love struggle with depression. Parents often feel discouraged and despondent during this stage because they believe that they have failed at their most important job—raising a healthy and happy child.

With support and encouragement, however, most parents eventually come to understand and accept the situation. They realize that while serious, depression isn't hopeless; instead, it is a very treatable illness, though one that they and their children may have to live with for a long, long time.

Some parents also go through one more stage: advocacy. Not only do they work hard to help their child get the best possible treatment, but they reach out to offer help and support to parents going through similar experiences.

Until moms and dads come to terms with their child's depression, however, many are consumed by guilt, anxiety, and shame. The guilt develops from self-blame: "Maybe it's my fault," Mom might think. "After all, I did drink a little wine when I was pregnant." Or she might say, "I always suspected problems in my family. I never knew my uncle, but people always said he was a sad person. Maybe he was depressed; maybe it runs in my side of the family."

Additionally, parents often feel a kind of retrospective guilt. Depression is rarely diagnosed right away; when parents first suspect a problem, they usually take their child to the pediatrician who finds no physical reason for the child's disturbing behavior and may say something like "Let's wait a few weeks and see if the symptoms go away." Some parents interpret this to mean that the child is to blame for his "bad" behavior. If he is lethargic, for instance, they believe that he's deliberately being lazy; if his grades slip, it's because he isn't trying hard enough. Later on, when the depression is diagnosed and parents learn their child is suffering from a real illness, they feel guilty. As one mother explained, "I would never blame him for having chicken pox or pneumonia. But with depression, that's what I did. I blamed my child for getting sick—which makes me feel awful."

Parents' anxiety often manifests itself in worries about the future. They might think, "Okay, the antidepressant the doctor prescribed seems to be working, but what if she stops taking it. Will the depression come back? And if it does, what will her future be like? Will my other children get depressed too?" If their child is suicidal, parents wonder if they can keep their child safe or if by some oversight on their part the youngster will try to hurt herself again.

Joyce, forty-two, knows the agony that parents can undergo. When her daughter, Rebecca, was fifteen, she was an honor student, class officer, soloist in the school choir, and an "all-American girl who never gave us a moment's trouble," Joyce says. "But a few months into her sophomore year, we got a call from her guidance counselor who told us that several times within the past few weeks, Becky had suddenly started crying in class. When we asked our daughter what was wrong, she said, 'It's like sometimes I can't find myself. I can't find the person I used to know; I look in the mirror and all I see is this ugly, unhappy girl and I get really scared. Sometimes I feel so bad I just have to cry.' "

At about this same time, Becky's grades began to slip; she went from being an A student to failing several subjects, all within a few short months. Then one evening when Joyce, her husband, Stan, and their seventeen-year-old son, Howie, were sitting down to dinner—Becky was supposed to be at choir practice—the phone rang. It was the police; Becky had been arrested for shoplifting.

At this point, Joyce and Stan brought their daughter to a psychologist recommended by the school. "But things only seemed to get worse," Joyce recalls. "Becky told the psychologist that if things got too bad she was going to swallow some mercury she kept in her backpack [the youngster was a lab assistant at school and had access to many chemicals]. The psychologist told Becky that because he felt her life was in danger, he'd have to tell us. Becky said if he did, she'd run away. Well, he did tell us and Becky did run away." Joyce and Stan drove all over town looking for their daughter; two days later, an exhausted Becky appeared on their doorstep.

But the situation continued to deteriorate. Becky's psychologist felt she needed further evaluation and referred her to a psychiatrist, who concluded that Becky was acutely suicidal. He recommended that she be hospitalized to ensure her safety. So for the next several years, Becky went in and out of various hospitals and treatment programs. Doctors also prescribed a number of different antidepressants, which appeared to have little effect; eventually, in fact, she was labeled "treatment resistant." Finally, after trying to inhale the contents of a fire extinguisher, she was admitted to a state hospital.

Joyce recounts the enormous emotional toll Becky's odyssey took. "It changed me forever. A black cloud always hovered overhead. I never knew what new horror a phone call or letter would bring. I would go out and see a mother shopping with her teenage daughter and my heart would break because I felt I had lost that with Becky and I would never have it again.

"My husband was very supportive, but there even came a point when he said, 'I can't take it anymore. I need a break.' So for two months, I made the four-hour drive to the hospital by myself. I felt like I was put into this little box and the door was closing. And there was nobody out there who understood.

"I looked to place blame. I searched to find what I could have done to cause this. Like I remembered that when Becky was growing up we had moved several times because of my husband's job. Now I wondered, 'Could that have done it? Could that have hurt her?' After a year of this, I was physically and emotionally wiped out. And I felt guilty that I had robbed my son of some of his childhood. He completed high school when Becky was hospitalized, and even though my husband and I went to the graduation, I knew we were just going through the motions. Every ounce of our attention and energy was being channeled into coping with Becky."

After a great deal of searching, the family finally found a small, residential treatment program for Becky, and the clinicians there helped her and her family get the help and support they needed. After a year, Becky improved enough to move to a group home where she still lives, making slow but steady progress. Now twenty-five, she has finished high school, is taking college courses, and is enjoying a part-time job teaching music at a senior citizens' center. Her parents, too, are feeling better—and certainly more hopeful.

Admittedly, Becky's situation is more extreme than most. As I've said earlier, not all depressed kids get suicidal or run away from home. But I offer this story because it so vividly illustrates many of the emotional reactions and difficulties parents may experience when dealing with a depressed child.

- **How Depression Affects Couples**

Liz, now forty-six, admits that dealing with her son's severe depressions pushed her and her husband to the brink of divorce. From the time their son, Ethan, was five years old, the couple had been struggling with his frequent bouts of debilitating depression. "We felt so much anger toward each other," Liz says. "We blamed each other, especially when we thought about the life we had expected to have and the life that we did have because of our son."

That life was marked by frequent, weeks-long periods of depression during which Ethan would become extremely irritable, sleep twenty hours a day, and refuse to eat or to leave the house. "We could never go out because we were terrified that if he was alone, he'd hurt himself or his sister," says Liz. "And when we were home and he was in one of his depressions, we would feel as if we had to walk on eggshells. He was just miserable to be around. You would never call him bad, though—just very, very sad."

Finally, the relationship between Liz and her husband, Jake, got so rocky that they decided to separate and went into therapy to prepare for their breakup. "But after a while, we realized that we didn't really want to be apart; what we wanted was to learn how to cope better with our son. Once we refocused our attention and concentrated on that, things got better for us." Together, the couple learned as much as they could about depression and its treatment and joined a local support group. "We really became 'experts' in depression which helped us to feel empowered," says Liz. "We no longer felt at the mercy of a medical system that was telling us what was best for our son. We knew who the good doctors were, what the most promising treatments were, and how we could get our son the best treatment available. Today we even lead support groups for other parents struggling with depressed kids." Now twenty years old, Ethan is much better—and so, happily, is Liz and Jake's relationship.

But not all couples fare as well. I've known a number of couples whose marriage was irreparably damaged by the stress of dealing with a depressed child. Blame is one major reason why. If Mom and Dad have different parenting styles, one usually believes the other caused the child's depression by "not spending enough time with him" or "spending too much time with him," or "overprotecting him" or "not shielding him enough" from life's disappointments and losses. Dad will fault Mom for going back to work too soon, or for hiring an incompetent nanny; Mom will blame Dad for being too rough on their child or placing too many demands on him. Parents who suspect a genetic predisposition toward depression often point accusatory fingers at each other's families, saying things like "This is your fault; you're the one with all those crazy relatives!"

Sometimes problems arise when parents interpret their child's symptoms differently. For example, Dad may believe that his daughter's refusal to get together with friends is a sign of depression and decide that she needs professional help, but Mom may insist it's just the child's way of getting more attention, and that taking her to a therapist would be an expensive and time-consuming overreaction.

In some instances, a child's depression may exacerbate unresolved problems between the parents. One couple I recently worked with have a ten-year-old son who is clinically depressed. Apparently, the mother wanted to have another child years ago, but the father refused, and for years the mother has been harboring deep resentment about it. Many times in the course of our discussions she has said, "I know this wouldn't have happened if Josh had a brother or sister. But my husband wouldn't hear of it and now I'm forty-five and it's just too late!"

Grace and Gordon, whose twelve-year-old son, Kyle, suffers from depression, offer another example. The family had lived near the mother's parents for several years. It was a comfortable arrangement; the grandparents were willing and happy baby-sitters, which allowed Grace to go back to nursing school and the parents to have an occasional night out. When Gordon's job forced them to move to another state, however, Grace had to leave school. The new community had no nursing program within commuting distance, and Grace resented having to forsake her career goal. When Kyle was diagnosed with clinical depression two years later, she insisted that the move—"which was my husband's idea"—was to blame.

■ **How Depression Affects Single Parents**

Single parents experience many of the concerns and emotions that married parents do. But there is a special twist: They often worry that their single-parent status may have contributed to their youngster's emotional problem.

But let me say this: In my clinical experience, I have not found childhood depression to be any more common in single-parent families than in intact, two-parent families. That does not mean, however, that single parents don't feel some extra stress and strain.

For example, the circumstances that often lead up to becoming a single parent—divorce, abandonment, unwed pregnancy, or the death of a mate—already put a parent under increased stress, which may affect her (or his) ability to cope effectively with the child's problems. Other single-parent worries like "I haven't had enough time to spend with her," or "He needs more men as role models in his life," or "All the caregivers I've had to leave her with must have been over-whelming" can also cause strain.

Another common source of stress for single parents centers on treat-ment, since it almost always involves regular therapy sessions for the child, and, often, for the family as well. Not only is this expensive—increasingly, even families with insurance find strict limits placed on reimbursement—but it is also logistically difficult. Chauffeuring chil-dren to and from school and doctors' appointments, and coordinating efforts to support your depressed child both at home and at school is simply tougher for one parent to shoulder than it is for two.

▪ How Depression Affects Families Coping with Divorce and Remarriage

Dealing with depression is always difficult, but when parents divorce and/or remarry and form new stepfamilies, some special issues can arise. For instance, just as intact couples tend to blame each other for their child's illness, so do separated and divorced moms and dads—only their emotions may be more intense because they're often fueled by the hurt and anger that precipitated and followed their breakup.

Such blame is often tied into the custodial arrangements. I recently spoke with the divorced parents of Casey, a ten-year-old I started treating for clinical depression. During our conversation, Casey's mom, who had recently remarried, accused her ex-husband of ignoring their child during custodial visits: "Casey says all she does is sit in front of the TV and watch videos when she stays with you. And you're always late with your child support. And what about camp for her this summer? You promised she could go, then claimed you couldn't afford it."

Casey's dad returned fire, claiming, "I think the problem is yours.

Your new husband is too strict with her. She's feeling suffocated by him and all his rules. She says living with you is like being in the army!" Clearly, problems between this couple escalated and became magnified as they tried to deal with the custodial arrangements concerning their depressed child.

Stepfamilies are also affected by a child's depression, but with a few unique stressors. For instance, depression often can intensify the underlying allegiances and alliances within a stepfamily. So one stepparent might say to the biological parent of the depressed child, "He's your son. You deal with him." In many stepfamilies, only the biological parent actively participates in the child's evaluation and treatment. While this may strengthen the bond between them, it can drive a wedge between the stepparent and the depressed child, as well as between the parents themselves.

Daryl, age seven, was diagnosed with depression when he was six—only a few months after his mom had remarried. Before Mom and her second husband had had time to adjust to being a married couple, Daryl and his mother found themselves spending hours together in therapy—without Daryl's new stepdad. What's more, Daryl's illness brought his biological father back into the picture in a more active way—which added more strain to the situation.

Although understanding and supportive, Daryl's stepfather became resentful of all the attention his wife was paying to Daryl's emotional needs and the time she now was spending with her ex-husband. What's more, having his mom and dad together, even if it was only in therapy sessions, fueled Daryl's fantasy that his "real family" might be reunited. On some level, he felt that the only thing preventing this reconciliation was his mom's remarriage, which increased the tension between Daryl and his stepdad.

Limited therapy time did not allow us to deal with all the issues that arose in this family, but we tried hard to help Daryl accept the changed circumstances of his life. In part, we did this by using therapy sessions to replicate the dynamic that had occurred in Daryl's life. That is, first we met with him and his biological mom and dad. Next we worked with Daryl and his mother, and then separately with Daryl and his father. Finally, we worked with Daryl, his mother, and his stepfather. This approach eventually helped Daryl accept the reality of his parents' divorce and his mother's remarriage. It also helped strengthen his relationship with his biological father. What's more, sorting out these issues proved effective in alleviating much of Daryl's longstanding depression.

■ How Depression Affects Healthy Siblings

A child's depression can affect her brothers and sisters in a number of ways, often depending on the age and developmental stage of the healthy sibling. Babies and toddlers may become upset by the emotionally charged atmosphere of the family home, though of course, they can rarely put that into words. (In fact, young children are so sensitive to family changes that they are often effective emotional barometers, picking up a problem before parents or other relatives do.) Preschoolers may become confused and angry by their depressed sibling's behavior—all of a sudden big sister Amanda doesn't want to play anymore or starts "acting mean."

As parents, then, you want to be very sensitive to the needs of your healthy toddlers and preschoolers. Spending extra one-on-one time with them, and making sure they get to spend plenty of time with other, happy kids—through play dates and other social activities—are very important for children this young.

Older children, from school-aged to teens, experience a broad spectrum of emotions when a sibling is depressed. For instance, they often feel a strong sense of guilt, as if something they did or said caused their sibling's problem. Twelve-year-old Diane knew that she was her parents' favorite: a popular, bright student, she was always being singled out for honors and awards. She was, as her mother was fond of saying, "our special blessing from God." When her fourteen-year-old brother was diagnosed with clinical depression, Diane felt it was her fault. "He was always getting in trouble, getting bad grades, being sent to detention. And my parents were always comparing us; I was the 'good child,' David was the 'bad.' I don't know, but, well, maybe David got sick because of me, because I made him look bad—not on purpose, you know, but because I never got in trouble."

Jimmy, a fourteen-year-old with hemophilia, also felt responsible for his ten-year-old sister's depression. "If I didn't cause it, I sure didn't help. It's like I was always getting all the attention from everybody because I had to go to the doctor all the time or to the hospital. And Rosalie was always 'over there,' somewhere in the corner, like she didn't exist or something. She got sadder and sadder. Maybe there are other things that were wrong with her, I don't know. But if Mom and Dad hadn't always been bothering with me, maybe they could have had more time for her."

Sometimes healthy children feel a kind of survivor's guilt. They wonder, "Why did I get to be happy and healthy when my brother is always so sad and unhappy?" Occasionally, these healthy siblings begin to show signs of depression themselves. Sometimes, that's because depression runs in the family. But it may also be because developing depression can be a way to get into the family spotlight. Though unaware of their motivation these kids develop depression in order to get Mom's and Dad's attention redirected to them.

Many siblings also feel a sense of sadness and loss when their brother or sister is diagnosed with depression, particularly if they are exceedingly close to the ill child. Having a sibling with depression represents a loss of the happier way things used to be.

Trisha, age thirteen, is a case in point. She was devastated when her sister Rochelle, just fourteen months her junior, became depressed. Says Trisha, "My sister was my best friend. I love her more than anybody, even though we used to fight over silly stuff, sometimes. But then when she got depressed, we weren't that close anymore. She never wanted to talk or to go shopping or anything.

"Sometimes she made me really angry because when she acted that way she got lots of attention. She even got to go to a special school, and she didn't get in trouble even when she messed up. But most of the time I just feel so sad. I miss the way things used to be between us."

Trisha also worries that she might develop depression, a concern shared by many healthy siblings. They think, "If my sister can get so sad maybe I can, too."

Another interesting—and, for parents, extremely frustrating—way in which depression can affect siblings is that it can spur them on to try to reestablish the family's equilibrium. Here's how this can work. If the depressed child becomes withdrawn and mopey, the healthy child, unconsciously uncomfortable with and frightened by this change in his brother or sister, becomes overactive and aggressive in a misdirected effort to keep the family on a level plane. Sometimes, this reaction occurs for a different reason. The healthy child may become overly energized as a way to encourage his sibling to snap out of his depression. In a sense, the healthy child is simply trying to get things back to normal.

Occasionally, though, the stigma of his sibling's depression may make the child extremely angry, ashamed, and eventually, even depressed. Once word of the depressed child's problem gets out into the community—which often happens when there is a public incident like a runaway or suicide attempt—the healthy sibling may be taunted by the other children in the neighborhood. As one nine-year-old brother of a depressed teenager confided to me recently, "The kids in school all tease me. They say 'Your brother's crazy! He tried to off himself.' I feel bad for my brother, but sometimes I feel like he's ruining my life!"

While living with a depressed sibling affects school-aged children and teenagers in much the same way, adolescents often confront two additional issues. First, if the teenager is the oldest child in the family, her parents, laboring to cope with the problems of their depressed child, may expect her to act as a surrogate parent for her younger brothers and sisters. The teen may have to cook, clean, and get the younger kids to do their homework, take their baths, and keep their dentist appointments. And while a certain amount of such "parentification" is okay—teenagers often like to feel that they are helping their family in a time of crisis—too much is burdensome and can lead to serious emotional problems.

Of course, teenagers aren't the only ones that can become overly parentified; I've seen this happen to siblings as young as seven or eight. But when there are several brothers and sisters in the family, the spillover from parents often falls onto the oldest.

The second special problem teenaged siblings face centers on parents' becoming overly protective. All moms and dads worry about their teenager's growing demands for independence. They know they need to let them explore the world on their own, but they often feel anxious as they hand over the keys to the car or extend the curfew to midnight. But parents who are dealing not only with a teenager but with another depressed child tend to become overly cautious and controlling. These parents may view any teenage moodiness as cause for alarm, and if a single grade slips slightly, they may worry that it's a sign of a deep emotional problem.

Teenagers resent this extreme protectiveness. And parents need to know that while they are right to be attentive and concerned—after all, depression does tend to run in families—hovering too closely won't prevent the problem. But talking with your teenagers about your concerns can help. You can say something like "I don't want to be sitting on top of you and mess in your life, but I want you to know that if you ever feel overwhelmed and don't know what to do, or feel like things are getting out of control, then you can come and tell me. I promise to listen and not get mad. And if you don't want to talk to me or your Dad, you can always talk to Aunt Susan or Uncle Charles or your coach at school."

How to Minimize the Impact of Your Child's Depression on the Rest of Your Family

There's no way to avoid all the repercussions a child's depression will have on your family. Daily routines will get disrupted while your child undergoes treatment, parental energies and attention will get shifted toward meeting the demands of the depressed child, especially during times of crisis, and family members will inevitably feel some guilt, sadness, anger, and resentment. But having a depressed child doesn't have to overwhelm you or your family. The following tactics can help you keep a sense of balance and perspective.

- *Become an expert.* Learn as much as you can about depression, including its causes, risk factors, symptoms, and range of available treatments. Also find out what community resources are available to you and your family, in terms of education, treatment, emotional support, financial assistance, and more. Educating yourself and your family helps lessen fears and eliminate misconceptions, and makes it easier for you to cope. (For a list of organizations that can provide additional information on depression, see the "Helpful Organizations and Resources" section at the back of this book.)

If you're comfortable with computers and have access to the Internet, there's lots of valuable information on depression available in cyberspace. For example, the National Alliance for the Mentally Ill (NAMI) has a site on the World Wide Web (http://www.cais.com/vikings/nami) that lets you tap into additional resource material. If you subscribe to any of the commercial on-line services, you open up many other electronic sources of information and support. Through CompuServe, you can access IQuest, which offers more than 450 health and medical databases; the Healthnet reference library; and the Parents Forum, where moms and dads exchange information and ideas on a wide variety of subjects. NAMI also has a bulletin board on America Online with sound information on children and depression. Prodigy allows you to plug into the Medical Support Bulletin Board, where depression is one of the topics. In addition, users also can meet weekly in a "chat room" to talk with others live. There's also a Parenting bulletin board, similar to CompuServe's Parents Forum. (Note: The kinds of information and resources available electronically are growing every day. Consider these suggestions a starting point for your own networking and research. And for more electronic resources, see the "Helpful Organizations and Resources" section at the end of this book.)

- *Expand activities and relationships outside of the family.* Encourage your healthy children to get more involved in activities that don't center on depression or illness—things like sports, art, music, or involvement in religious or community groups. And do the same for yourself. You and your family need to take part in fun pastimes that will serve as a diversion so that dealing with a child's depression does not become all-consuming.
- *Ask for help.* Sometimes coping with a depressed child is more than a one- or even two-parent job. It may mean enlisting the support of

other adults—usually friends or relatives—to help you and your family manage. For instance, you may need another trustworthy adult to care for your other kids when you have to take your depressed child to therapy sessions, or to help you accomplish those household errands and chores you don't have time for when your depressed child is having behavior problems which require constant attention, such as frequent temper tantrums or overly aggressive actions toward other children.

Friends and relatives can also be a great source of comfort. Sharing your feelings with an understanding and sympathetic friend can help lighten the load of coping with a depressed child. But if you have trouble asking for help, feel you're overburdening your confidants, or just want a more objective person to talk to, seek professional counseling for yourself. Seeing a therapist is not an admission of weakness; you're dealing with some very tough issues that could make anyone feel confused and overwhelmed. Short-term supportive counseling may be just what you need to get your bearings and move ahead with your life.

- *Rid yourself of guilt.* While it's important to look squarely at your own possible contribution to your child's problem and to acknowledge and try to change any of the attitudes or behaviors that you think may be harmful, blaming yourself for your child's problem isn't fair or useful. Remember, your child's depression is an illness that needs treatment. It is not a punishment for or consequence of poor parenting.

- *Set realistic goals.* Understand that while your child is recovering from depression, the pace of his achievements may be slower than you might hope. For example, if your child's grades have dropped from A's to C's, don't expect them to bounce back up right away. Instead, look for more gradual improvement—a few B's among the C's, for instance. Unrealistically high goals set you and your child up for failure and disappointment and risk exacerbating the depression. Setting more realistic goals, however, will help you and your child feel positive and optimistic about his progress and keep you heading in the right direction.

Don't forget to set realistic goals for your nondepressed children as well. Sometimes, when a child becomes depressed, his healthier siblings are made to feel that they have to be extra good—do all their chores, keep their grades up, never come home late or cause their parents any concern—to make up for the problems surrounding the depressed child. But setting such perfectionistic goals puts too much pressure on your kids. And if they don't live up to those expectations, their sense of failure can damage their sense of self-esteem and put them at risk for depression.

- *Try not to feel stigmatized.* Although mental illness doesn't have quite the stigma it used to have, it would be naive to suggest that you won't encounter any prejudice. Your kids may get teased about having a "crazy" brother or sister; other adults may wonder what you did to "make" your child depressed.

  Feeling stigmatized can be quite painful, but it doesn't have to be devastating. If your kids are being teased, explain that the problem is not with them, but with the people doing the teasing. You can say something like "I know it hurts when people say mean things about your brother, but they do it because they don't understand depression. You know that we are doing all we can to help your brother, and that it's your job to keep doing what you're doing—going to school, doing your homework, playing with friends, and having fun. The important thing is to remember we love you and we'll always be here to take care of you."

  If other parents make hurtful or blaming remarks to you, remember this same advice. Also, don't feel obligated to defend yourself and your parenting to anyone else, particularly casual acquaintances. Remember, your child's depression is not your fault and you don't owe any explanations.

- *Sharpen your communication skills.* Parents coping with a depressed child need to be able to talk with one another, to honestly share their thoughts, fears, anxieties, and hopes that surround their child's illness and treatment. This is as true for intact marriages as it is for couples who are separated or divorced. Failing to communicate about your child's treatment will lessen his chances for rapid and complete recovery.

- *Join a support group, or start one if there's none available.* Parents and siblings of depressed children often tell me that they feel isolated and alone, as if they're the only ones in the world who are coping with these problems. But that's simply not true. Thousands of other moms, dads, brothers, and sisters know exactly how you feel—they've been there themselves. Sharing feelings and concerns with them goes a long way toward helping you feel less alone. The sense of camaraderie and support can be an enormous help in dealing with your depressed child.

As I've mentioned, friends and family members can be a warm and welcome informal source of support. But if you want something more structured, your local mental health association or one of the national associations listed in the "Helpful Organizations and Resources" section of this book will help you find a support group near you.

There is one particularly effective source of support that merits special mention—the Journey of Hope, an education and support program that helps families dealing with mental illness. Launched in 1992, the program now operates in thirty-two states and two provinces of Canada. Its family education component consists of a twelve-session course for families of individuals with severe and persistent mental illness, including clinical depression. The course focuses on the skills and knowledge you need to cope more effectively with your mentally ill relative. The support-group component offers families ongoing emotional support and practical advice from other people dealing with similar problems and experiences. (To find out how to reach the Journey of Hope, turn to the "Helpful Organizations and Resources" section.)

In addition to seeking emotional support from others, you need to do a few more things to help yourself. Specifically, you need to take occasional time off from chauffeuring your child to therapy appointments, educating yourself about depression, and catering to your child's many needs to concentrate on yourself. So have dinner with a friend, go to a movie, or take a brisk walk around the park. If you can take some time to care for yourself, to recharge emotionally and physically, you will be much better able to help your child.

■ *Love the child you have.* As we've already discussed, having a child who suffers from depression can be very disappointing, so it's natural and normal every once in a while to mourn the loss of the child you thought you'd have. But accepting your child as he is now is important for his happiness and for yours. As the mother of one depressed pre-teen commented, "If I could offer some advice to other parents, I would just want to remind them that there's nothing more precious than the child you have. The child you may have imagined you would have—the one with no problems, worries, or cares—isn't real. But the child you have is very real. So love him and be there for him. Just be there."

When a youngster becomes depressed, the entire family experiences a range of feelings and situations that test the emotional health and resiliency of every member. While the stress can tear families apart, it can also bring them together. With compassion, sensitivity, aware-ness, energy, commitment, and skill in balancing everyone's needs—including your own—your family can become closer and stronger than ever before.

Chapter

6

Kids Who Want to Die:

Childhood Depression and Suicide

Children commit suicide—a frightening and terribly sad fact. It's estimated that every year over two thousand teenagers kill themselves, making suicide the third leading cause of death (following motor vehicle accidents and homicide) among adolescents. Between 1980 and 1992, the rate of suicide in this age group climbed 120 percent, according to government statistics.

A widely cited survey conducted by the George H. Gallup International Institute in 1994 revealed that 5 percent of American children ages twelve through seventeen said they had attempted suicide at least once. Interestingly, while teenage girls *attempt* suicide more often than teenage boys, more boys actually *succeed* in killing themselves.

It's not just teenagers who are taking their own lives; suicides have been reported in children as young as five, although the incidence of suicide increases significantly in adolescence. Nonetheless, in 1992 alone 314 suicides among children ages five through fourteen were reported by the National Center for Health Statistics.

These statistics are very disturbing. But what's even more alarming is that they probably far underestimate the real numbers because we cannot accurately tally the number of children who think about, attempt, or commit suicide. How many teenagers who die after drinking and driving are actually victims of suicide? How many unsuccessful suicide attempts are unknown to anyone but the child himself? (Studies of suicidal kids reveal that anywhere from 60 to 85 percent of parents were unaware of their children's suicidal behavior.) Some experts believe that childhood suicide is nothing short of an epidemic.

The methods children use in their suicide attempts are wide-ranging. Most kids turn to guns, but hanging and the deliberate ingestion of poisons or pills are also fairly common. And very young children often attempt suicide by running in front of cars or trains, slashing their wrists with razors or knives, or jumping from high places.

As chilling as this information is, nothing drives home the tragedy of childhood suicide more than the experience of a real child. Nine-year-old Teddy is one youngster I will always remember.

For the first four years of his life, Teddy was a fairly happy child. He had a mother and father who loved him and each other, and a younger sister whom he adored. Early on, his preschool teachers pronounced Teddy "gifted"; he had a very high IQ and was charming, gentle, and sensitive.

But soon after Teddy turned four, his father suddenly died of a heart attack. Following his death, Teddy's mother became more and more depressed and withdrawn. Though she had been only a social drinker, alcohol now became the chief focus of her life.

With his mother drinking so heavily, Teddy assumed the caretaking role in his family in the months and years following his father's death. He straightened up the house, prepared the meals, and made sure his younger sister got to school on time. As he got older, he even kept track of the family bills and worried about their finances. The family didn't have much money; his mom had lost her job, and the family survived on his dad's life insurance and survivor's benefits. Through it all, Teddy continued to do well in school, although his teachers noticed that he had become a sad child who seemed to have the weight of the world on his shoulders.

One night when Teddy was nine, his mother went out drinking and didn't come home for two days. Panicked, Teddy telephoned his uncle, who reassured him that his mother would return but did nothing to find her. By the time his mom came back, Teddy was distraught and losing control. He took a pistol from his father's gun collection, held it to his heart, and in front of his mother, pulled the trigger. Fortunately, it didn't fire, but his mother, shocked and frightened, rushed her son to the emergency room.

That night Teddy was admitted to the children's psychiatric ward. In the hospital, the doctor asked him why he'd tried to hurt himself. Teddy answered in a near whisper: "I didn't know what else to do. I asked God to help me and he didn't lift a finger. I felt bad all the time; I had to get it to stop."

Depression: A Major Risk Factor for Suicide

Like young Teddy, children often attempt suicide to end intense emotional suffering. And while not all suicidal children suffer from depression—and not all depressed children attempt suicide—studies show that depression significantly increases a child's risk. In fact, research reveals that children with mood disorders like depression are more than five times more likely to attempt suicide than children not affected by such problems.

But, you might ask, can children of only six or seven—kids who are still too young to understand fully the concept of death—seriously attempt suicide? Well, for years we didn't think so. But as clinicians and researchers began to look more closely at suicidal youngsters, they began to realize that having an inaccurate understanding of death—even believing that death is temporary and reversible—didn't mean you couldn't be suicidal. Any child who perceives suicide as a way to solve a painful personal dilemma—whether to end his suffering, to join a deceased loved one "in heaven," or even to gain attention—is at increased risk.

Other Risk Factors

Depression is not the only risk factor for suicide, however. Several other emotional and situational factors also exist and put children in increased danger. Not surprisingly, there is considerable overlap between the risk factors for depression and suicide. But let's briefly explore each one as it specifically relates to the latter.

■ Emotional Factors

PREVIOUS SUICIDE ATTEMPT

We've already discussed the fact that the biggest risk factor for depression is a previous episode of depression. Similarly, a child who already has attempted suicide is much more likely to try to kill himself in the future than a child who has never made an attempt.

HOPELESSNESS

As in adults, children's feelings of hopelessness—despair, a belief that they have no control over themselves or their surroundings, and a sense that things just won't get any better—can predispose a youngster to suicide.

EATING DISORDERS

We already know that a child with an eating disorder is at risk for depression. Correspondingly, adolescents suffering from bulimia and anorexia nervosa seem to be at higher risk for suicide.

SUBSTANCE ABUSE

Work with children—particularly teenagers—who chronically use drugs or alcohol has revealed that these kids are often significantly depressed and are using the substances to dull their pain. Taken in sufficient quantities, alcohol actually can induce or intensify a child's depressed state and raise the likelihood of suicidal behavior. Substance abuse also increases that youngster's risk for self-destructive behavior because it can reduce inhibitions and, therefore, boost the chance that the child will express his suicidal thoughts through such life-threatening behavior as drinking and driving.

PSYCHOSIS

Children suffering from psychotic illness, especially those who hear hallucinatory voices telling them to hurt themselves, are at increased risk for suicide.

■ Environmental (Situational) Risk Factors

FAMILY HISTORY

For several reasons, a child's risk for suicide dramatically increases if his parent or other close relative has attempted to kill himself. Just knowing that a loved one committed suicide puts the act within the realm of possible behaviors, allowing the child to think, "If my Dad can commit suicide, so can I."

The suicide of a loved one, particularly a parent or sibling, also triggers lots of powerful feelings in children, including anger and guilt. Such a sudden and untimely death often leaves the surviving child with unfinished emotional business, like not having a chance to make peace after a quarrel or to say good-bye. Often, when this child experiences another loss later in life, the unresolved feelings resurface and can make her more vulnerable to depression and other emotional problems which, in turn, can raise her risk for suicide.

Additionally, some researchers believe that suicidal children have a distinctive biochemical makeup—abnormalities in the way their brains manufacture serotonin and other neurochemicals—that is genetically inherited. This, too, could explain why a family history of suicide puts a child at greater risk.

STRESSFUL LIFE EVENTS

Studies of suicidal children show that most have experienced extremely stressful events—witnessing intense violence, undergoing an extended hospitalization, surviving a natural or man-made disaster—which increase the likelihood of suicide. This doesn't mean that stressful occurrences will drive a child to suicide. Rather, it suggests that these events predispose a child to an emotional problem—particularly depression—which increases his risk.

SIGNIFICANT LOSSES AND SEPARATIONS

The loss of a loved one through death, divorce, separation, or abandonment can trigger a sense of worthlessness, rejection, loneliness, and poor self-esteem in children. These negative emotions increase the risk for self-destructive behavior, including suicide.

PHYSICAL OR SEXUAL ABUSE

Children develop a sense of trust in the world from the positive, nurturing relationships they have with early caregivers, particularly parents. Eventually, children internalize these feelings; they feel a sense of security inside themselves as well. But when that all-important early bond between caregiver and child doesn't form or is ruptured—as often happens with abused children who cannot trust their caregiver—that sense of security and safety is not internalized. The abused child comes to view the world as a scary, unsafe place, and to see himself as a rejected, unworthy, helpless, and vulnerable victim. Such a damaging self-image can lead to self-destructive behavior, including suicide.

POOR ACADEMIC PERFORMANCE

If a child repeatedly fails in school, he can begin to suffer from a diminished sense of self-esteem, especially when school performance is considered by the child and his parents as a means of evaluating self-worth. This is particularly true for children who feel powerless to remedy the situation, as revealed in such statements as "I just can't do any better"; "I guess I'm too dumb to learn."

POOR PEER RELATIONSHIPS/SOCIAL ISOLATION

Children who feel they don't "fit in" and who don't enjoy healthy, positive friendships with other kids are frequently at increased risk for suicide. The social and emotional challenges of childhood and adolescence often prove overwhelming to youngsters who don't have the strong support of good, close friends.

FAMILY CONFLICT OR DISCORD

Severe discord between mothers and fathers can put their child at increased risk for depression—as we already discussed in chapter 2—and accordingly, heighten the likelihood that the youngster will become suicidal. Such intense conflict usually means that parents and other relatives have not developed effective communication and problem-solving skills to help work out difficulties and cope with stress. Instead, they have likely acquired maladaptive ways to cope with difficult situations.

Children living in such tension-filled environments often adopt these maladaptive and sometimes self-destructive ways to cope with stress, which puts them at greater risk for suicide. For example, the fourteen-year-old who breaks up with her boyfriend may get involved in reckless sexual behaviors; the eighteen-year-old who gets rejected from his first-choice college may decide to blow off steam by drinking and driving.

HEARING ABOUT OTHER SUICIDES

Some children may even be able to be "talked into" suicide. There is some evidence to suggest that when troubled youngsters hear about the suicide of others, their own risk for suicide rises. Reports have shown that the number of teenage suicides climbs for the week or two immediately following the suicide of another adolescent and the publicity that surrounds the tragedy. This frightening phenomenon has even earned its own label—the "cluster effect"—and has thrown the effectiveness of suicide prevention programs, which try to head off suicide by talking about it, into doubt.

David Shaffer, M.D., professor of psychiatry and pediatrics at Columbia University College of Physicians and Surgeons, has done a good deal of work on adolescent suicide prevention. He says that "although there are anecdotal reports of individual youngsters committing or attempting suicide after attending suicide prevention classes, this has never been documented in a systematic fashion." But his research *does* suggest that suicide curricula in high schools—the most popular prevention method among children in the United States today—*do not seem to influence troubled teenagers for the better.* Specifically, these classes do not make the adolescents more likely to seek help. In fact, troubled children who participate in suicide prevention classes that give them more information about suicide actually find these classes distressing.

My own opinion is that it's important to create an environment in the school where children can speak openly, comfortably, and confidentially to a trained adult about their anxieties and concerns. But blanketing the school with prevention curricula *without also focusing on individual counseling* may well have the adverse effect of increasing the risk of suicide in vulnerable children.

To be fair, some suicide researchers dispute the whole notion of the cluster effect. And clearly, more research needs to be done. But to be safe, I would recommend that if your child learns of the suicide of someone with whom he identifies—another teenager, friend, classmate, or role model such as a teacher, sports figure, actor, or even rock star—*and* your child already shows some symptoms of depression or is at increased risk for suicide, you should be on the alert.

Sexual Orientation as a Risk Factor

Homosexual or bisexual teenagers are up to three times more likely to attempt suicide than heterosexual children, according to the Hetrick-Martin Institute, an organization that focuses on the special needs of gay, lesbian, and bisexual youth. However, neither documented research nor my clinical experience leads me to believe that sexual orientation in and of itself makes a youngster more vulnerable; instead, increased risk seems more related to problems homosexual adolescents experience in coming to terms with their sexuality.

Homosexual kids must wrestle not only with the usual identity crises and struggles for independence common to all teenagers, but also with society's stigmatization of anyone who is not heterosexual. So at the same time these youngsters are beginning to feel attracted to individuals of the same sex, they are hearing about and witnessing homophobia in all its many forms, from unkind stereotyping of and jokes about homosexuals on TV sitcoms to unprovoked, violent attacks on gay men and women in real life.

These kids don't want to be feared and disliked, and they certainly don't want to lose the respect and love of friends and relatives. But they often find it difficult to hide or suppress their sexual needs and desires. When homosexual or bisexual children feel ashamed, confused, different, and socially isolated, it's hard for them to develop the kind of self-esteem and resiliency they need to defend themselves against the emotional problems, particularly depression, that increase their risk for suicide.

Suicide's Red Flags

Although there is no "typical" suicidal child—which makes it hard to predict whether or not your youngster actually will make an attempt—there are some common warning signs. These are:

- **Suicidal "Ideation"**

   We already know that thoughts of suicide, statements about suicide or about the desire to harm themselves, and self-destructive themes revealed in play or drawings are often signs of depression in children. Popular wisdom says that individuals who talk about suicide never go through with it; but that is simply not true. In fact, children who talk about suicide—making such remarks as "You won't have to put up with me much longer," "I wish I were dead," or "I just can't stand living like this anymore"—are clearly at risk for suicide.

   Research conducted by Cynthia Pfeffer, M.D., chief of the child psychiatry inpatient unit at the Westchester Division of New York's Cornell University Medical Center, reveals that a child who thinks about suicide is at more than three times the risk for future suicide attempts than a child who does not have suicidal or self-destructive thoughts. So if your child seems preoccupied with death—frequently talking about death and dying, drawing pictures or playing with death as a theme, or listening to music or watching videos that focus on death—stay on the alert. He may well be considering suicide.

- **Final Arrangements**

   Pay close attention to a child who starts giving away cherished belongings, such as favorite CDs, books, or jewelry, writes a farewell letter or a will, or says good-bye to friends and family members with finality—"Thanks for everything you've done for me; it's meant a lot." It may indicate that she is making arrangements to die.

- **Acting or Talking As If No One Cares; Giving Up on Themselves and Others**

   Kids who repeatedly say things like "I feel as if I'm all alone. Nobody really cares if I live or die," or "I'm trouble. This family would be better off if I had never been born" may well be communicating suicidal intentions.

■ **Sudden Cheerfulness After a Prolonged Period of Depression**

One of the oddest and most confusing things about suicide is that depressed children often make an attempt when they are starting to feel better. But there's a reason for that. When a child is deeply depressed, she is often so immobilized that she can't even think through the act of killing herself. But once she starts viewing suicide as a way out of her suffering, that very thought—and the sense of power and control it gives her over her life—can lift her mood.

■ **Having Frequent "Accidents"**

Lots of accidents are chance events or unavoidable consequences of dangerous circumstances. A child involved in Peewee football is a lot more likely to come home with bumps and bruises, for example, than a child who spends his afternoons in the library or in front of the computer. But when multiple incidents occur in very close proximity to each other—your six-year-old keeps running across the street without looking even though you've taught him how to cross safely, your ten-year-old repeatedly falls out of the big tree in your backyard, your sixteen-year-old totals the car two or three times in just as many months—it may be a sign of a serious emotional problem, an unconscious expression of self-destructive or suicidal thoughts.

■ **Engaging in Dangerous or Risky Behavior**

Kids who repeatedly engage in risky behavior like playing with matches or knives, climbing to precarious heights, drinking and driving, experimenting with illicit drugs, or engaging in unsafe sex— even if they don't come to any harm—may be expressing deep-seated self-destructive wishes or suicidal thoughts.

Suicide's Triggers

In children who are vulnerable to suicide, certain circumstances can serve as immediate triggers for an attempt. Here are the most common.

- *Heartbreak.* This includes rejection by a loved one, loss of a parent, and, in teenagers, breakup with a boyfriend or girlfriend.
- *Trouble with the law, or possible disciplinary action.*
- *Arguments with parents.* Everyday bickering probably isn't going to precipitate a suicide attempt, even in a vulnerable child. But arguments in which youngsters feel severely denigrated or humiliated can lead to suicidal behavior.
- *Altered state of mind.* Drinking alcohol or taking illicit drugs often checks an individual's inhibitions. This increases the likelihood that the youngster will act on his impulses and engage in dangerous and self-destructive behavior.

One last point: Even if a child is at high risk for suicide, she cannot kill herself without two things: *an available method*—for example, access to a gun, poisons, pills, or sharp objects such as a razor blades—and *opportunity*, that is, the privacy to attempt suicide. This is why suicidal children need to be under extremely close watch twenty-four hours a day.

What You Can Do

If you believe that your child may be at risk for suicide, is actually considering it, or has made an attempt, there are several steps you can take:

1. *Seek immediate professional help.* Call your child's therapist (if he's already in treatment) or pediatrician and make arrangements for an immediate evaluation of the situation. You can also call a mental health center or suicide hotline (phone numbers are listed with

operator information or in your telephone directory), or take your child to a hospital emergency room. Just remember: *Suicidal thoughts and actions are very serious and should always be viewed as a medical emergency.* Postponing action for even a few hours can mean the difference between life and death.

2. *Eliminate the means.* Remove any weapons, rope, or sharp objects from your home, or lock them away. If you (or your spouse) own a gun, make sure it's kept unloaded and secured in a safe place, that ammunition is locked and stored separately from it, and that your child has no access to either the gun or the ammunition.

   Be sure to lock away all medications—both prescription and over-the-counter—as well as poisons, including seemingly innocuous cleaning fluids (kids have been known to attempt suicide by drinking liquid bleach and household detergents). Let your child know that you are taking these steps because you love her and want to keep her safe.

3. *Respect your child's feelings.* Once your child has been thoroughly evaluated by a mental health professional and you are sure that she is not in any immediate danger, you can lower her risk for suicide by showing respect for her feelings. Instead of trying to argue your youngster out of her emotional state with comments like "Oh, come on. Things aren't as bad as all that," offer sympathy and support with words like "I know you feel really angry and upset right now. This must be really hard for you."

4. *Maintain open communication.* Make it clear that you are always ready and willing to listen to and talk about whatever may be troubling your child, including suicidal thoughts. Let your youngster know that she can always come to you or another trusted adult if she feels any self-destructive impulses and that you will do your best to get her the help and support she needs.

Keep in mind, though, that suicidal kids often deny their feelings and self-destructive intentions. So you have to not only keep alert for signs and symptoms but also to follow up on your suspicions until you can either confirm or correct them.

Courtney's parents learned that lesson well. While they had noticed that their twelve-year-old was spending more and more time alone in her room, had become quite irritable, and had let her grades slip from B's to D's, they blamed these changes on preteen moodiness. One day, though, while Courtney's mom was putting away the laundry, she found a bottle of prescription painkillers—left over from when she had an abscessed tooth removed—in the back of her daughter's sock drawer. When she asked Courtney about the pills, the youngster said, "I had a headache the other night and I thought I'd hold on to them just in case it got worse."

Mom's internal warning light flashed on, and she brought Courtney to see me. After interviewing the youngster carefully, I discovered that Courtney had been having suicidal thoughts for over six months, and that she had even formulated a number of specific plans to kill herself, including taking an overdose of pills or "falling" in front of a subway train. These self-destructive thoughts were very scary to Courtney. In reviewing the family history, I also learned that depression ran in Courtney's family; her maternal aunt had once been hospitalized for depression and her mother had been in treatment several years ago.

I advised her parents to lock all pills and sharp objects out of their daughter's reach, which they did immediately. In addition, I arranged to see Courtney twice a week and started her on an antidepressant. After she got over her initial nervousness about being in therapy, Courtney relaxed a bit; she felt greatly relieved that she could talk about her feelings with someone who would not judge or reprimand her. She also used drawing to help express and explain some of her recent thoughts and impulses. During one session, she drew a picture of her own funeral, which depicted an organist but only one mourner in attendance.

After three months of individual treatment, Courtney was doing much better. Her depression began to lift and she was no longer suicidal. But her parents remained vigilant and ready to act quickly if any warning signs appeared.

A Note of Hope

Thinking about suicidal children isn't easy. The subject is complex and emotionally charged, even terrifying. But remember: Even if your child is suicidal, there is hope. Identifying the earliest warning signs of depression and/or suicidal tendencies and getting your youngster immediate help and appropriate, effective treatment will significantly increase your ability to keep your child safe and well.

Chapter

7

How to Find Help:

Choosing the Right Therapist for Your Child

Bringing my child to therapy was incredibly hard. First, I had to acknowledge that he had a problem and that wasn't easy. I felt like I had messed up, like it was my fault. Second, I had to find a good therapist. But how do you do that? Who do you turn to? How do you know if he's any good? Then, there were the finances. How much would it cost? Could we afford it? Here we were, a couple with four young kids, struggling to make ends meet and faced with this enormous expense. It was the biggest responsibility I ever felt.

—Ellen R., whose son was
diagnosed with depression at age seven

By now you know a good deal about why children develop clinical depression, and you have become more alert to the many symptoms that may signal this disorder. You also understand more about how depression affects not only your child, but your entire family as well. Additionally, back in chapter 3, I offered specific guidelines as to *when* you should consult a mental health professional for your youngster.

Now let's discuss *how* to get your troubled youngster the kind of help he needs and deserves.

How to Find the Right Therapist

If you suspect that your child is depressed, one of the most important things you can do is begin searching for the right therapist. Admittedly, this isn't easy. There are lots of mental health professionals to choose from, and selecting the best one for your youngster can be confusing and intimidating. But if you can break this task down into smaller, more manageable steps, you'll be able to find a qualified, affordable, and effective therapist for your depressed child.

- **Know Who's Available**
First, let's consider who's out there. Most therapists fall into one of three broad categories: psychiatrists, psychologists, and social workers.

Psychiatrists are physicians—which means they've completed four years of medical school—who have also undergone at least four years of postgraduate training. In addition to training in adult psychiatry, child and adolescent psychiatrists like myself have completed a special two-year fellowship program specializing in young children, adolescents, and their families. One of the advantages of working with a psychiatrist is that his medical training gives him expertise in all possible treatment alternatives, including medication when appropriate.

As you try to locate a psychiatrist for your child, you'll probably hear the terms *board eligible* and *board certified*. In this context, "board" refers to specialized certification exams given by the American Board of Psychiatry and Neurology. A board-eligible psychiatrist has met all training criteria necessary to take the exams, while board-certified psychiatrists have taken and passed these tests.

Although many excellent psychiatrists are not board certified, the credential is considered a significant qualification. Board certification is often a requirement for psychiatrists to be on the medical staff of many hospitals; further, some insurance companies only provide reimbursement for treatment by a board-certified physician. To find out whether the psychiatrist you are considering is board certified, you can contact the American Board of Psychiatry and Neurology. (The address and phone number are listed in the "Helpful Organizations and Resources" section.)

Another choice of therapist is a *psychologist*. Today most psychologists with their own practice have earned a doctoral degree in psychology, although some states still require only a master's degree for licensure. Because they're not medical doctors, psychologists can't prescribe medication. But that shouldn't deter you from choosing a psychologist if you find one you and your child like and trust. Psychologists often work closely with psychiatrists and other physicians who can offer additional expertise and consultation if and when medication is needed.

The third broad category of therapist is the *social worker*. Preferably, you want to find a clinical social worker, a mental health professional who has earned a master's degree in social work, has undergone years of clinical supervision, and is licensed and/or certified by the state. Many states require clinical social workers to continue their education and training to keep their license or certification.

Although clinical social workers don't undergo training that's as extensive as that of psychiatrists or psychologists, many are talented individual and family clinicians. Often, too, clinical social workers' fees are lower than psychiatrists' or psychologists', so you may find them more affordable. To locate a clinical social worker in your hometown, contact the National Association of Social Workers (see "Helpful Organizations and Resources").

Depending on which state you live in, psychiatrists, psychologists, and social workers may not be your only options. You may also have access to a variety of other therapists, including child analysts (usually but not always psychiatrists trained in psychoanalytic theory), psychiatric nurse practitioners or clinical specialists, mental health counselors, pastoral counselors, marriage and family therapists, and drug and alcohol counselors. Some states have licensing or certification procedures for these therapists, but criteria vary from state to state.

■ Get a Personal Referral

Because there are so many different therapists out there, it's always best to begin your search with a personal referral from your family doctor, your child's pediatrician, school counselor, or school psychologist. You can also ask a member of the clergy or other professional who frequently deals with families and children. And, of course, a trusted friend or relative is also a good resource.

Another way to find a qualified therapist is to contact professional organizations. Call or write, briefly explaining your child's problem and requesting a referral to someone in or near your hometown. Among the most helpful of these professional groups are: the National Alliance for the Mentally Ill, also known as NAMI (state and local affiliates use the name Alliance for the Mentally Ill or AMI); the American Academy of Child and Adolescent Psychiatry; the American Psychiatric Association; the American Psychological Association; and the National Association of Social Workers. (To contact any of these organizations see the "Helpful Organizations and Resources" section.)

Still another alternative is to get in touch with local organizations, including family service agencies, community mental health clinics or centers, hospital psychiatry departments and outpatient clinics, state and local medical and/or psychiatric societies, private clinics or employee assistance programs at your workplace. Any of these groups can help you find a good therapist for your child.

■ Check Licensing

Make sure that the therapist you choose is licensed or certified by your state. It's important. A license means not only that the therapist has had formal training and/or passed any required qualifying exams, but also that he is subject to some form of state regulation and review. For example, most states have procedures for considering complaints regarding the clinicians they license. The state can impose limitations on the scope of the clinician's practice if a pattern of complaints emerges, or it can suspend or revoke his license.

(Note: State licensing or certification is different from board certification. State licensing requires that a therapist meet the criteria determined by the individual state in which he wants to practice; board certification means that the therapist has met criteria and standards of practice set by a national professional board. I would never recommend a therapist who is not licensed by the state, but I would recommend a good therapist who is not board certified.)

In practice, a state license isn't a guarantee that your therapist will be effective, but it definitely increases your chances of finding someone who is qualified and ethical. Usually, a licensed therapist will display his certificate in his office. If you don't see it, ask. If you're uncomfortable asking, call your state's Department of Health, Office of the Secretary of State, or appropriate professional organization (e.g., if the clinician you're checking is a psychiatrist, call the American Psychiatric Association; for a psychologist, call the American Psychological Association). Ask how you can contact the state agency in charge of professional licensing so that you can find out whether or not your therapist has this critical credential. If you want to know whether a clinical social worker you're considering is licensed, call the American Association of State Social Work Boards (listed in the "Helpful Organizations and Resources" section), which will refer you to the proper licensing agency in your state.

■ **Investigate Special Expertise**

A license is not the only criterion you should use in choosing someone to work with your child, nor is the category of therapist to which the clinician belongs. Just as important is the individual therapist's area of expertise and his experience in working with children the same age as your child.

Obviously, you want to find someone who knows a great deal about childhood depression. But if you and your spouse have divorced, your depressed child might be better off with a social worker who specializes in divorce than he would be with a child and adolescent psychiatrist whose focus lies in psychopharmacology (treating people with medication). If you have an alcohol problem in your family, you want to find a clinician who has a great deal of experience and training in the special problems of alcoholism to work with your depressed child.

■ **Understand Treatment Costs**

If you have health insurance, your policy may cover some or all of your child's treatment. However, many such insurance plans require high co-payments or deductibles, which means that you will be responsible for a large part of any bill. Other policies restrict the choice of "covered" therapists to a preselected panel.

Navigating today's managed-care maze isn't easy. That's why it's important to get accurate information concerning what your insurance will and will not cover and exactly what procedures need to be followed in order to be eligible for reimbursement. For example, some HMOs (health maintenance organizations) may require you to get an initial referral from your child's primary health care provider (pediatrician or family practitioner) before they will approve reimbursement for mental health treatment. To find out how your plan works, read the description of benefits that came with your policy. If you have more questions, call the subscriber information department associated with your policy or plan—and don't give up until you get an answer you understand.

Unfortunately, not all insurance policies or plans provide adequate mental health coverage or access to the best therapists. If you are not happy with the alternatives offered, you may need to go outside the plan to have your child see the therapist of your choice. In such cases, you will have to pay out-of-pocket for your child's treatment. The same is true if you have no health insurance. So be sure to discuss fees with the therapist in advance. Ask about sliding-fee scales based on your income and ability to pay, or make arrangements to pay your bills over time.

Funding for treatment may also be available through your child's school, particularly if your child's depression is interfering with his academic performance or classroom behavior. In most cases, therapy will be part of a comprehensive program called an Individual Education Plan (IEP) designed with your input and assistance. Once the IEP is approved, its components, including therapy, can be paid for by the school system. (This process is governed by federal laws and regulations designed to ensure that every child has access to an appropriate public education. For more information, contact NAMI at the address listed in the "Helpful Organizations and Resources" section of this book.)

■ Trust Your Instincts

No matter how much you admire and respect the person or organization that referred you to a specific therapist, listen to that little voice inside yourself before making a final choice. One mom I know wishes she had trusted her instincts before entrusting her child to Dr. A. Even though it's been years since her daughter, Emily, now twenty-five, was in therapy, the memory lingers. As this mom recalls, "Finding a therapist for my eleven-year-old daughter was overwhelming. I wound up taking her to the first person another mother I really respected recommended. But from the start, I didn't like this doctor. All he ever seemed to do was point out Emily's flaws; he never noticed how bright and charming she was. Week after week, I would sit in his dimly lit waiting room while my daughter was having her session and feel totally excluded. He never talked to me, he never saw the family together. I would never have tolerated this from my own doctor, but this was my kid and I felt very vulnerable, like the situation was completely out of my hands. After a year of this and of seeing only marginal improvement, I finally switched doctors and brought Emily to someone we both felt good about. The difference was amazing. After a few months, her depression began to lift, and over the next year she became a happy child once more. Today, she's graduating from veterinary school and is a normal, well-adjusted adult."

Emily's mom would be the first to agree that for treatment to work, you need to find a therapist whom you like and trust. And that's a matter of personal preference; the therapist your best friend swears by may strike you as cold and distant—or vice versa.

You also need to find someone with whom your child feels comfortable, as Karen learned. Suspecting that her six-year-old son, Timmy, was suffering from depression, she took him to a well-respected psychologist. But before each session, Timmy would kick up a storm. As Karen remembers, "He'd cry and plead, 'Don't make me go. I hate that guy! He doesn't understand anything. All we do is play stupid games. Please don't make me go!' I felt terrible forcing him, but we felt it was in his best interest.

"When I talked to the doctor about it, he told me that Tim's upset was a good thing, that he was displacing his anger at us onto him and that that was an important part of the therapeutic process. But I never felt good about that. And it never got any better. For six months, he'd go through the same hysteria before each visit. Finally, I said 'enough' and took Timmy out of treatment which was unfortunate, because he suffered from depression for years. Only when he went to college and got into therapy with someone he trusted did he start getting better. But I'll never forget what a miserable bad time we had when he was young."

Most kids experience several ups and downs in treatment, and many do feel some anger or resentment toward their therapist at various points in the process. But if your child consistently protests treatment, take note. Speak to the therapist and carefully consider his explanation and advice. But if you don't feel right about it—and if the problem persists—seek a second opinion.

Ideally, you want to shop around, getting the name of at least two or three therapists and meeting with each one personally. Most therapists charge for such consultations, but I believe that a face-to-face session is the best way to determine how comfortable you and your child are with the therapist, how easily you both can communicate with him, and how confident you are of the therapist's ability to help your child. (Getting a good look at the waiting room is helpful, too, especially if your child is very young. The offices should be well lit and child friendly, with some kid-sized furniture and a few toys or books designed to keep children relaxed and occupied while they're waiting for the therapist.)

Increasingly, however, as mentioned, insurance companies and HMOs are limiting your choice of therapists to certain preselected clinicians. But even in this situation, you can usually exercise some choice, even if it's only among this select group.

You could also go outside the system or find a therapist affiliated with a community mental health center or clinic. Some therapists charge on a sliding-scale basis, which generally means that the less you earn, the less you pay. No matter what your financial situation, though, try hard not to settle for a therapist with whom you and your child don't have a good connection.

Sizing Up a Potential Therapist

Once you've contacted a therapist (or therapists), you want to get a clear sense of his credentials and qualifications as well as his therapeutic and personal style. Here are twelve important questions to ask during your initial consultation.

1. What is your training?

In many states, anyone can call himself a psychotherapist. He doesn't have to have any special training—or any schooling at all, for that matter. He can simply—and legally—hang out a shingle or list himself in the Yellow Pages and start seeing patients.

For that matter, even if you got to an individual who calls himself a "psychiatrist" you're not assured of getting a therapist who is specially trained in mental health. In many states, for instance, all anyone has to do is graduate from medical school to call himself a psychiatrist or other medical specialist. So be sure to ask the clinician you're considering what kind of professional education he has had.

One more tip: Training at a prestigious institution doesn't necessarily make someone a wonderful therapist or, more important, the right one for your child. On the other hand, I would not recommend working with a "psychotherapist" who got his degree through a mail-order correspondence course. Before making a commitment to any therapist, always ask yourself, "Do I feel comfortable entrusting my child's health and well-being to this person?"

2. Are you licensed or certified to practice by the state?

We've already discussed the importance of licensing; it's intended to protect you, the consumer, by limiting licensure to individuals who meet the state's criteria for education and training in a particular field or specialty.

There's no reason to feel uneasy asking a therapist if she's licensed. A good therapist will not feel threatened; in fact, she will welcome the question because it lets her know that you are a concerned and informed consumer. But if a therapist you are considering does balk at this query or becomes evasive in answering it, find someone else for your child.

3. How long have you been practicing?

Many parents prefer a therapist who has been practicing for many years. Understandably, they believe that the more experience the therapist has, the more effective he will be. As a general rule, that's true, but remember that in some cases, a more recent graduate may be just as effective as a seasoned professional if not more so. For instance, since using antidepressants to treat depressed children is a relatively new approach, some younger psychiatrists are more familiar and comfortable with this form of treatment than are clinicians who did their medical training twenty or thirty years ago. So don't automatically discount a therapist you otherwise like because you're worried that he's too young.

4. How would you describe your clinical approach?

You want to know more about the way this therapist approaches her patients. Does she focus mostly on individual therapy with the child, or does she generally work with families? Does she believe in treating certain children with medication or is she strictly against it? If you have a family history of depression and your relatives have been successfully treated with medication, you may want your child to work with a psychiatrist who will consider this kind of treatment. On the other hand, if your child is dealing with a lot of family-centered issues, a psychiatrist who specializes in medication (also called a psychopharmacologist) may not be the best choice.

Many if not most clinicians will tell you that they are eclectic in their approach, using a wide range of treatment methods. That's perfectly fine. In fact, it's often preferable. Because there's no single effective treatment for depression—no magic bullet that helps every depressed child—you want to work with someone who is skilled and flexible enough to draw on many techniques and to tailor treatment to the individual needs of your child rather than one who tries to fit your child's problems into a single, rigid approach.

5. Have you treated many children like mine before?

Since kids change so much from year to year, you want to find a therapist who has had experience in treating youngsters of your child's age. A therapist who specializes in adolescents may not be the best choice for your six-year-old, just as a clinician who works almost entirely with preschoolers and school-age kids may not be the most effective choice for your sixteen-year-old.

You also want to find a therapist who has treated children with problems similar to your child's. A depressed youngster might be better off working with a therapist highly knowledgeable about depression than he would working with someone whose focus is on drug and alcohol problems.

6. How long do you think treatment will take?

Every child is unique and no reputable therapist is going to tell you exactly when your youngster will be "cured." But you're not asking for that. You want only to find out whether this therapist views your child's treatment as short-term—lasting a few months or so—or a years-long process.

In part, the length of treatment depends upon the therapist's orientation. For example, a cognitive-behavioral approach is usually shorter than psychoanalysis. But having some indication of treatment length gives you a better idea of what you and your child are getting into and what kind of a commitment you will need to make.

It also gives you a way to compare therapists. If one tells you therapy should last two years and another says six months, ask each to explain the reasons for their estimates; then you can decide which feels right for you and your child.

7. When you worked with children with problems similar to my child's, what was the outcome?

Answers to this question will help you learn more about how these other children did—to what extent they were helped, whether they had recurrences or if they completely recovered. Of course, no therapist can guarantee a particular outcome, but you'll get a better sense of the clinician's experience.

8. How much will treatment cost?

Therapy bills can mount quickly, so right from the start you want to have some sense of how expensive your child's treatment could be. Along these same lines, feel free to ask other financial questions like "Do you have a sliding-scale fee policy? Will you bill my insurance company directly or do I pay you and then wait for reimbursement? Are you affiliated with any HMOs or managed-care organizations? Do you accept Medicaid?"

You can ask if your particular insurance company will cover the costs, but most therapists won't be able to tell you because plans vary so widely. As discussed, you're better off calling your insurance company, HMO, or managed-care organization to find out exactly what it will and will not pay for.

9. How will my family and I be involved in the treatment of my depressed child?

Many therapists primarily work alone with their young patients and have limited involvement with parents and siblings. But I believe that it's important for the therapist to understand and evaluate the family environment of every child in treatment. In most cases, I include parents in occasional therapy sessions and I'm always available to answer questions and address concerns.

10. How will I be kept informed of my child's progress?

Don't allow yourself to become so intimidated by the therapist or the therapeutic process that you relinquish your rights and responsibilities as a parent. No one cares more about your child's well-being than you do.

So ask the therapist whether she will keep you informed of your child's progress via telephone calls, face-to-face meetings, or written reports, and how often you can expect to hear from her. If you're not comfortable with the response, say so, and try to work out a feedback schedule that will suit you both.

11. What arrangements do you have for after-hours crises?

Problems don't always arise during regular office hours, which is why you need to find out if and how the therapist can be reached in an emergency. Most therapists have some sort of contingency arrangements in place, whether a beeper system or on-call coverage, so that you can get help fast during a crisis. Make yourself familiar with these arrangements right from the start, *before* an emergency occurs.

12. How will you coordinate care with any other health care professionals working with my child?

Often children, particularly those who require medication, work with a variety of clinicians, including a pediatrician or family doctor, a nonmedical mental health professional, and a psychiatrist. They all need to communicate with one another regularly to discuss your child's progress and any changes in his treatment. For this reason, some parents prefer to find a therapist who is part of a group practice where most if not all your child's clinicians work in the same building and have frequent and easy access to one another.

You also want to make sure that the therapist you choose takes enough time to answer all your questions and seems genuinely interested in the welfare of your child. So if by the end of your initial meeting you don't feel confident in a particular therapist's abilities and hopeful about the outcome of the treatment, keep looking.

Changing therapists once your child begins treatment often causes many problems. For one thing, leaving a therapist brings a new loss to a child who may well have experienced too many losses already. For another, it may trigger additional negative emotions; your child may feel that he "failed" therapy, or that his inability to work with the therapist was all his fault. So choose a therapist with care. Eventually, you'll be able to find the right clinician for your child.

Making a Diagnosis

The therapist you choose will probably spend the first one or two sessions evaluating your youngster's problem. He'll observe your child firsthand and conduct detailed interviews with her, with you and your spouse, and, sometimes, with other important family members or caregivers. He'll also obtain your child's social, academic, developmental, and medical history, along with your family's health history.

At this point, most therapists begin to develop a "differential diagnosis," or initial range of diagnostic possibilities. Over the next few weeks or months, they systematically narrow down the diagnosis as they work with the patient, getting to know him better through first-hand interaction and observation.

Occasionally the therapist may also ask you and/or your child to complete formal diagnostic tests or symptom-rating checklists to help him make an accurate assessment. Literally hundreds of these tests exist, including such self-report measures as the Children's Depression Index, Short Children's Depression Inventory, and the Children's Depression Scale, where children themselves may complete unfinished statements or identify statements that best describe their feelings. Additionally, there are interview tests—including the Kiddie-SADS (Schedule for Affective Disorders and Schizophrenia for School-Age Children) the Interview Schedule for Children, and the Children's Depression Rating Scale—in which the therapist asks the child and, occasionally, his parents questions about themselves and their behaviors.

Of all diagnostic tools available today, however, one of the most widely used is the Child Behavior Checklist (often called the CBCL), developed by psychologists Thomas Achenbach, Ph.D., and Craig Edelbrock, Ph.D. First published in 1978, the CBCL offers a list of over 100 statements to which parents are asked to respond. There are several versions of the test, including one for parents of children ages two to three; another for parents of children ages four to eighteen; and a self-report test for youngsters on at least a fifth-grade reading level. So, for example, the parent will read the statement "My child complains of loneliness" or "My child seems sad" and then answer whether that comment is always, sometimes, or never true.

The CBCL helps the therapist identify clusters of behaviors that may suggest depression as well as a whole range of other emotional problems. It helps the therapist gain a more complete picture of all your child's difficulties so that he can put together an effective and comprehensive treatment plan. But one of the main reasons the CBCL is so popular is that it is a fairly simple, straightforward tool with questions that are easy to answer. And it allows the therapist to make useful comparisons. Parents and children can be asked similar questions; then the therapist can compare their responses to see if they are viewing the problem differently.

The CBCL can also help identify differences between how each of the child's parents views a particular problem. For instance, if Dad says his son is having lots of problems and Mom sees none, this is important information for the therapist to have. Such insight will help him more accurately pinpoint whatever is causing or exacerbating the child's problem.

Additionally, the therapist can compare his patient's responses to those of other children of the same age and gender. This helps give him a frame of reference on how much of your child's behavior is normal for a child of this age and gender. (Remember, the way depression looks is often different for boys and girls.)

During the evaluation period, many therapists will also want to contact your child's school and teachers. With your permission, he may ask the teacher to fill out a standardized checklist like the special teacher version of the CBCL. The therapist may also want to arrange a meeting with your child's teacher (again, with your knowledge and permission), or even observe your child in her classroom. That way he can get a better sense of how your youngster interacts with her teachers and classmates, and understand how the school setting may be contributing to her problem.

Some parents worry that getting teachers involved with their youngster's treatment may cause their child to be labeled "disturbed" or "a problem." But remember, your therapist will want to involve the school only if that's where many of your child's problems have surfaced—which means that in all likelihood, your youngster's behavior and performance have already alerted her teachers to a problem. Incorporating their opinions and perspectives will only increase the chances that your child's treatment will be successful.

Give It Time

As a parent, you naturally want to know *exactly* what's troubling your child. And you may expect the therapist to give you a clear, definitive diagnosis *right away*.

But as you can see, arriving at an accurate diagnosis takes time; it is a complex and not always exact science. One reason for this, as we discussed in chapter 4, is that a child may have more than one disorder at the same time, such as depression and an anxiety problem. Another is that a child may have an underlying depression that is difficult to detect.

Within the first few sessions, however, the therapist should be able to offer a clear diagnostic picture of your child's problem. With your input and support, he will then develop and outline a specific treatment plan. But before agreeing to that course of treatment, be sure that you thoroughly understand the diagnosis and feel comfortable with the therapist's opinions and recommendations. And once again, if the therapist cannot explain why he came to a particular conclusion—or you have nagging questions about its accuracy and validity—seek a second opinion.

Chapter

8

How to Find *More* Help:

Getting the Right Treatment for Your Child

I get sad when I get in trouble. It happens a lot. I feel mixed up and confused, like I don't know what's going on. I feel better when I talk to my doctor. He doesn't get mad and he helps me figure stuff out.

—Jacqueline, age nine

Let's assume that you've found a therapist you trust. She has evaluated your child and arrived at a diagnosis of clinical depression. At this point, she'll work with you to develop a treatment plan designed to help your depressed child as much as possible, as quickly as possible.

Keep in mind that there are literally hundreds of different therapies available to treat depression today. The kind of treatment the therapist will recommend will depend upon her assessment of your youngster's symptoms and her own training and orientation—that is, the treatment approaches with which this therapist feels most confident and comfortable. What follows is a brief rundown of the major categories of therapy that are used to help depressed kids.

Psychodynamic Psychotherapy

Psychodynamic psychotherapy typically involves a series of individual sessions between the therapist and the child. In them, the therapist uses a variety of techniques to help the child express her thoughts, feelings, and fantasies, and to uncover hidden or unconscious ideas and conflicts that may be affecting her behavior. Helping kids make the connection between their unconscious emotions (like being angry at their big brother for getting cancer) and their actions (picking fights with other kids at the playground) often frees them up to behave and interact in a healthier manner.

Psychotherapy with adults (and often with adolescents) generally relies on talking about feelings and problems. Psychotherapy for younger children who often have trouble putting all their experiences, thoughts, and feelings into words takes a different form. In addition to asking the child direct questions and listening to her answers, the therapist uses more indirect methods to communicate, such as painting or drawing, encouraging fantasy play (often using puppets and dolls) in which the child can act out different life scenarios, or reading stories about characters going through similar experiences. For most young children, these methods offer less threatening and less scary ways to explore their innermost emotions.

When three-year-old Ruth was brought to see me, she was having difficulty sleeping, waking up three or four times a night because of "bad dreams." She'd also become an increasingly fussy eater; the only foods she would eat were Cheerios and chicken nuggets. Additionally, she had had a number of prolonged temper tantrums over the last few months.

During my first meeting with Ruth's mom and dad, they told me that their four-year marriage had become very rocky and that recently they had discussed the possibility of separating. But they did not see any relationship between their marital problems and their daughter's troubling behavior. They assured me Ruth was completely unaware of their difficulties; they took great care never to fight or argue in front of her.

During my first session with Ruth, I got a very different message.

When she entered my office, I showed her all the toys I had and told her she could play with whatever she wanted. Immediately, she went to the dollhouse and knelt down next to it. She picked up the father doll, put him inside the house, and then pushed him out through the front door saying, "Daddy going away. Goes out, out!" In her own way, she was letting me know that she knew very well what was going on in her family.

Such indirect communication also occurs in psychodynamic psychotherapy with older children. Jeremy, a thirteen-year-old who was showing many of the symptoms of depression, including appetite loss and persistent irritability, was reluctant to engage in any direct conversation during our first visit. Whenever I asked him a question, he answered with a curt, one- or two-word reply. Obviously, this approach was getting us nowhere.

So I took a different tack. Jeremy had told me that he was an avid comic book fan. So I asked him to bring some of his favorites to our next session. As we sat and read them together, Jeremy talked about the characters, pointing out which ones he liked and why he liked them, and the themes he most enjoyed reading about. Interestingly, Jeremy always favored loners who felt different and misunderstood or heroes who "got the girl." As we talked more, Jeremy's self-image as an outsider and his wish to be less shy around girls became apparent, although he could convey his thoughts and feelings only in this indirect way.

Central to my own approach to psychodynamic psychotherapy is the idea that every one of my young patients has a "story" to tell—a story that centers on his own unique perspective of the events and experiences in his life. I believe that getting depressed children to tell their story—in whatever way they can—is highly therapeutic and can help relieve their symptoms.

Listening to a child's story also helps me understand more about the roots of his difficulties, and the points at which he's gotten emotionally stuck. That way I can help a child understand that wishing that his baby sister would get sick and go away so that Mommy and Daddy could pay all their attention to him again didn't cause the baby's pneumonia and subsequent hospitalization. It also helps me assist a child whose healthy emotional development was derailed get back on track.

In some ways, the psychodynamic approach works more easily with kids than it does with adults. While it can be effective with grown-ups, they're often dealing with events that took place many years ago in their childhood, so it takes a great deal of time and effort to help them remember and reconnect. With children, emotionally significant events are much more recent, so it's often easier to get to the issues surrounding them. And since kids tend to be so emotionally expressive anyway, psychodynamic psychotherapy can often be a highly effective treatment for children with depression.

The psychodynamic approach isn't limited to individual therapy, however. It can also work with families, as we will discuss shortly. Additionally, psychodynamic therapy can be effective in groups. Older children who can talk about their fears, hopes, and anxieties with others who share these emotions often feel less alone.

Cognitive/Behavioral Therapy

Cognitive/behavioral therapy centers on the belief that the way children think about the events in their lives, the way they perceive themselves and the world around them, and their ability to solve problems strongly influence the way they feel and behave. According to supporters of this form of therapy, depressed children have developed incorrect ideas about themselves that have contributed to a poor sense of self-image. They tend to put a negative, self-deprecating spin on the events in their lives. If a child with depression invites a playmate to her birthday party and gets turned down, she doesn't stop to think that it may be because the would-be guest will be out of town that day or has a conflicting date. Instead the depressed child automatically assumes the worst, believing "she turned me down because she hates me" and that "she doesn't want to be my friend anymore."

Children with depression also tend to focus on the negative, even in situations that others would see as generally positive. One high school senior, for example, got six A's and one C on her report card. Instead of congratulating herself on her good grades, she spent the next several days putting herself down about the one weak mark. She also magnified the significance of the C—overgeneralization is a common trait in depressed kids—believing "Now I'll *never* get into college. No decent school will *ever* take me!" It didn't occur to her that studying harder or getting a tutor might help her raise her grade. Once a problem arises, the depressed child often sees no way to solve it.

Children with depression tend to blow negative events out of proportion and to minimize the significance of positive ones. When one depressed ten-year-old was voted "best all-around camper" by his counselors, he dismissed his parents' congratulations, saying "They just gave me that because I didn't cause them any trouble. Everybody has to get an award, and they probably couldn't think of anything else for me."

Depressed children tend to blame themselves when anything bad happens to them or to those they care about. Of course, self-blame is common in very young children who tend to be highly egocentric, seeing themselves as the center of the universe. A very normal three-year-old may well believe that his mother got sick because he was "bad." But if an eleven-year-old child thinks that way, she may have a real problem.

Through cognitive/behavioral therapy, the therapist works to recognize a child's negative thoughts and to understand how and why they are contributing to his sad feelings. The therapist helps the child learn to reevaluate events and see them in a different, more positive light. In short, the cognitive/behavioral therapist helps a child replace knee-jerk, self-defeating patterns of thought with more rational, optimistic ones. This, in turn, can improve the way your child behaves and feels.

One of the most important techniques in cognitive/behavioral therapy is attribution retraining. Instead of thinking "I failed the test because I'm dumb," the child learns to see that he failed the test "because I didn't study hard enough" or because "I didn't study the right material." The child also learns that in most situations he is not a helpless victim of circumstances, but someone who can exercise some control over his life. He learns to think, "If I study harder next time, I will be able to improve my grade."

Cognitive/behavioral therapists also help depressed children see events in their lives more realistically. Instead of believing that one C on a report card will keep her out of college, the high school senior learns to realize "It's just one grade. All my other grades are A's. And I am involved in lots of extracurricular activities that show I'm a leader in my school. I still think I have a good chance of getting into my first- or at least second-choice school."

Cognitive/behavioral therapists often encourage their young patients to do fun things that are simply incompatible with being depressed. For instance, many depressed children just want to sit around and dwell on their problems. But this behavior only makes them feel more depressed. Instead, doing things they might enjoy—like going to McDonald's, riding a bike, playing basketball with other kids, or meeting a friend at the mall—can help their depression to lift.

As we've seen, depression is often associated with disruptive behavior, including inappropriate expressions of anger. Part of the work of cognitive/behavioral therapy is to help kids modify such negative behaviors by using a variety of techniques. One of the most useful for young children is the Star Chart system. It works on the theory that children will change their behavior to obtain a reward.

To develop a star chart, the therapist helps the child identify one or two positive ways of managing or expressing troublesome feelings. Then a plan is designed in which a child can earn a star (or sticker or happy face, or whatever other symbol you and your child prefer) whenever he behaves in certain appropriate ways. Earning a preset number of stars brings the child various rewards. Five stars may earn a special snack; ten may mean a trip to the video store where he can select whatever movie he likes. (Make sure the goals you choose are attainable; setting unrealistically high goals will only make your child feel worse!) Representing the plan through an easily understandable chart that you can post on the refrigerator allows the child to track his progress. Here's an example.

Joey's Program for Putting Punching Feelings in a Safe Place

Joey is learning how to put punching feelings in safe places and how to put punches into words. Joey will earn a star when he puts punching feelings into a safe place. He will earn another star when he puts punching feelings into words.

Safe Places to Put Punching Feelings
1. Punching bags, pillows, mattress
2. Walking the feelings to the playroom or bedroom

Putting Punching Feelings into Words
1. I'm mad because . . .
2. I'm sad because . . .

Put Stars Here

Mon.   Tues.   Wed.   Thurs.   Fri.   Sat.   Sun.

5 ☆s = favorite snack   15 ☆s = trip to ball game
10 ☆s = pick a video   20 ☆s = new toy

One word of advice: If your child is happy and healthy, you may want to implement a star chart system on your own in order to help your child learn to behave better. And that's fine. But if your child is depressed, it's best to work with his therapist to create a star chart plan that addresses his special needs. In this way, the chart can help not only to change negative behaviors into positive ones but also to provide continuity between what's going on in therapy and what's happening at home.

Family Therapy

At the core of family therapy is the belief that families have the ability, with the assistance of a supportive and well-trained therapist, to heal themselves. In joint sessions with Mom, Dad, the kids, and other key family members, everyone can voice their opinions, sort out disagreements, and air their feelings in a safe, nonthreatening environment. The goal is for family members to open lines of communication and develop healthy ways of relating to one another. Bringing relatives together in family therapy takes some of the focus off the individual child, which in itself can help relieve some of the depressed child's symptoms.

The therapist works with family members to identify issues, interactions, and dynamics that may be contributing to your youngster's depression. For example, a child may become depressed in an unconscious attempt to keep his parents from getting a divorce by shifting concern away from their marital problems and toward himself. In other instances, the depressed child may be expressing symptoms on behalf of his family.

That's what happened in the M. family. Sixteen-year-old Lewis's suicide attempt finally jolted his father, an alcoholic, to enter a treatment center and get help for his problem. Once in recovery, his father's behavior became less erratic and more predictable. He stopped being so verbally abusive to Lewis and the rest of the family, including Lewis's mom and his two younger sisters. As Lewis's father began to deal with his own problems, his son's suicidal feelings gradually disappeared and his other symptoms began to lessen.

Family therapy is also extremely useful in uncovering unhealthy patterns of behavior that tend to repeat themselves from generation to generation. Suppose, for instance, that your own parent died when you were twelve, and that you went through much of your adolescence feeling abandoned, lonely, and withdrawn. You may have a tendency to re-create this experience as your daughter approaches adolescence by unconsciously—that is, completely unintentionally—encouraging negative thinking in your child and by not supporting her participation in social activities. As a result, your child may begin to become depressed—and, you may not even be able to realize it. After all, you say to yourself, "That's how I was when I was her age!" Family therapy can be very helpful in identifying—and breaking—these negative patterns.

Often family therapy emphasizes alliances between family members. In the L. family, for instance, four-year-old Vincent was so tightly connected to his mother that his father felt like an outsider, a situation that had created tension for the entire family. Through therapy, the family was able to identify and understand the impact of these alliances and to work toward achieving a more healthy balance among family members.

For the L. family, therapy sessions included not only talking about current issues but also having each parent talk about their experiences growing up. As it turned out, the father was the middle of three children, and he vividly remembered feeling excluded after his younger brother was born. In an unconscious way, the present situation—which once again made him feel like the outsider—was all too familiar, which exacerbated his discomfort and contributed to the tensions in the family.

One of the tactics that worked particularly well with this family was occasionally to change where everyone sat. Instead of always sitting close to his mother on a couch—with his father in a chair across the room—sometimes I asked Vincent to sit on the couch next to his dad, and his mother to sit in the chair. Other times, I'd ask Mom and Dad to sit together, which helped emphasize their relationship and their joint role as parents, and have Vincent sit next to his dad, which helped focus on strengthening the relationship between father and son. At home, I gave the family "assignments" that included having Vincent spend regular time alone with his father—going to a baseball game together, playing catch, running errands—while his mother used the time to do something she enjoyed but never seemed to have time for, like reading a novel or taking an exercise class.

While often highly effective in helping a depressed child, family therapy is not usually the sole course of treatment recommended. Frequently, I do individual psychotherapy with the child while another therapist works with the family.

(The reason I don't do both individual and family therapy involving the same patient is that I want to make sure that my one-on-one relationship with the depressed child remains pure, uninfluenced by any information or opinions I may hear in family therapy sessions. Although I periodically meet with the parents to keep them abreast of their child's progress, I include the depressed child in these sessions so that he never feels that I'm talking about him behind his back—but more about this later.)

Treating Depression with Medication

We all know that medication can be highly effective in treating adult depression. But as mentioned, in recent years clinicians have found that many of these same medications can help children with depression as well.

Nonetheless, there is legitimate concern—frequently noted in the media—about the increasing tendency to give medication to children for a wide range of behavioral and emotional problems, from mild hyperactivity to learning disabilities. I share the belief that no physician should prescribe medication casually or lightly. But I am firmly convinced that it can be an extremely effective and even life-saving treatment for many children with depression.

That said, however, let me also note that we don't have overwhelming, well-documented research to support what clinical experience has repeatedly demonstrated: that antidepressants can be effective in treating childhood depression. Thus far, studies have shown a puzzling but unmistakable placebo effect in children; that is, children given a pill made to look just like real medication but containing no active ingredients tend to do just as well as youngsters on actual antidepressants.

There could be several reasons for the wide discrepancy between research and practice. One is that the studies have been conducted with a relatively small number of children; therefore, the problem may lie in the studies' design or execution. Additionally, the children and families who have been involved in these studies tend to get a great deal of information about depression. And since we know that such education is an important element in effective treatment, it may well be that their increased understanding and awareness of depression may have helped all the participants—whether medicated or not— improve. Or it may simply be that depressed children in studies are finally getting the attention they've craved for so long, which in itself may help make them feel better.

There may also be a physiological explanation: It's possible that medications work differently in children's developing bodies from the way they do in adults'. However, since clinicians often see clear improvement in depressed kids treated with antidepressants, despite the inconclusive research, most child and adolescent psychiatrists— myself included—believe in using medication with certain depressed children.

■ When Medications Help

Treatment with medications isn't appropriate for all depressed kids. I tend to use it when the symptoms are largely physiological, such as sleep difficulties, appetite loss, or extreme lethargy. I also tend to prescribe medication when there is a family history of depression— especially when other relatives' depression has been helped by medication.

Another situation in which I use antidepressants is when a young- ster remains depressed despite individual psychotherapy and any changes made in the child's home, school, or family situation. But even then, I *never* rely on medication alone; instead, *I prescribe medi- cation only in conjunction with other forms of treatment,* like individual psychotherapy. Over and over, research and my own clinical experi- ence have shown that medication is most effective when it is used as part of a comprehensive treatment plan.

■ What You Need to Know Before Considering Medication

Never allow your child to go on medication until she has had a thor- ough medical checkup. One reason is that you want to make sure that the depression isn't related to or a symptom of another kind of medical problem, such as a thyroid condition or mononucleosis, both of which can cause some of the symptoms of depression. Also, since antidepressants can affect such things as blood pressure and body weight, measuring your child's height, weight, blood pressure, and pulse gives the doctor a baseline from which to monitor any changes. For similar reasons, your doctor will probably also want to run some blood tests on your child.

It's also important to have the doctor assess your child's motor coordination (noting whether or not he has any tics before taking any medications) so that the physician can see if any new ones occur once treatment has begun. And if the depressed child is an adolescent girl, the doctor would also be wise to do a pregnancy test, since some of these medications could affect the developing fetus.

When deciding whether or not to allow your child to be put on medication, be aware that antidepressants don't take effect immediately. It may take a few weeks to find the right dosage for your child. And it generally takes at least two weeks at this dosage to notice significant improvements. That's because antidepressants work by gradually and progressively eliminating depressive symptoms. Typically, the medications relieve physical symptoms first; for example, your child may begin to sleep better and to regain his normal appetite. Later you'll start seeing other changes in mood and behavior; symptoms such as crying and irritability will disappear. Finally, your child's attention span will lengthen, school work improve, and interest in activities return.

Once your child starts medication, he needs to be monitored regularly by a medical doctor (i.e., a psychiatrist, pediatrician, or family physician) who can check physiological changes. You and your child's therapist need to keep a close eye on any emotional and behavioral changes. If none of you notices much improvement within four weeks after your child reaches a therapeutic dosage, don't be surprised if your doctor suggests another kind of medication. Children are unique individuals; just because a certain medication works well for one youngster doesn't mean it's right for your child. So be patient. There are many effective medications available today. The chances are good that if one fails to help your youngster, another will work.

Placing a child on medication is a big decision—and it should be. All medications have their side effects, as we discuss in the next section. One issue you don't have to worry about, however, is dependency. The medications most often used to treat childhood depression are not addictive or habit-forming. As we've already discussed, you need to work with a doctor you trust and to make sure you understand and carefully consider the risks and benefits. Remember, though, the purpose of treatment is to relieve your child's suffering as quickly as possible—and for some children, medication really does help achieve that goal. If you're not comfortable with the doctor's recommendation, however, get a second opinion before giving your permission.

It also helps to know that most children won't always need to take medication. In fact, once symptoms are relieved, kids usually need to remain on medication for another three to nine months—possibly a year—before gradually tapering off, although some may need to continue longer. Keep in mind, however, that *no child should remain on medication for more than a year without his doctor considering a medication-free period* to assess whether or not he still needs such treatment.

▪ Antidepressants: A Closer Look

When it comes to treating children with depression, doctors tend to prescribe medications from the following major categories:

1. TRICYCLIC ANTIDEPRESSANTS (TCAs)

In chapter 1, we talked about the different causes of depression. As we discussed, sufficient levels of certain neurotransmitters (chemical messengers), specifically norepinephrine, serotonin, and dopamine, must be available between nerve cells to properly transmit the impulses that affect moods and emotions. Scientists theorize that reduced availability of these neurotransmitters can lead to, or at least make a child more vulnerable to, depression.

Tricyclics—which get their name from the three-ringed chain in their chemical structure—work by slowing down the process by which these neurotransmitters are reabsorbed by the brain cells. The TCAs increase the availability of certain chemicals between the brain cells, which helps to lift the depression.

TCAs reduce or even eliminate many of the symptoms of depression, including sad mood, sleeping problems, lethargy, and appetite loss. Among those TCAs most often prescribed for children are imipramine (brand name, Tofranil), desipramine (Norpramin), amitriptyline (Elavil), nortriptyline (Pamelor), and clomipramine (Anafranil).

These medications, usually given in pill form, are not addictive, so you don't have to worry that your kids will become "hooked" or dependent. But they can have certain side effects, ranging from such mild problems as dry mouth, constipation, headache, and weight gain or loss to more worrisome symptoms like an irregular heartbeat, increased heart rate, change in blood pressure, or seizures, particularly in kids with a personal or family history of heart problems or seizures. Before a doctor places your child on any TCA, make sure he is aware of any heart problems or seizures that your child or anyone in your family might have had. Many doctors will also recommend a baseline electrocardiogram (EKG) against which he can monitor any changes in the functioning of your child's heart. But because you're with your child every day, you need to watch out for any side effects your child may be experiencing and report them to the doctor.

One note: There has been a tiny number of reported cases in which a child has suddenly died while taking desipramine. But extensive research has failed to prove conclusively that the TCA was the cause. Nonetheless, as a result of these reports, clinicians are generally more cautious about using desipramine and other TCAs with children who have preexisting heart problems or a known family history of heart trouble. Considering the fact that millions of children have been helped by tricyclics, however—and that as a clinician I have found TCAs to be extremely effective in treating depressed children—I believe these medications are quite safe, particularly if the child is monitored carefully and regularly by a qualified physician.

2. SELECTIVE SEROTONIN REUPTAKE INHIBITORS (SSRIs)

In a sense, this newest group of antidepressants works similarly to TCAs—except that, as their name implies, they are more selective in their action, inhibiting the reabsorption only of serotonin. The best-known SSRI is fluoxetine, or Prozac, but other widely prescribed medications are sertraline (Zoloft), paroxetine (Paxil), and fluvoxamine (Luvox). Although both adult and child patients have reported some dry mouth, nausea, excess sweating, weight loss, and jitteriness among other side effects, many enjoy substantial improvement in their symptoms with few or no side effects at all. Due to their relative safety and limited side effects, SSRIs have gained rapid acceptance in clinical practice.

3. MONOAMINE OXIDASE INHIBITORS (MAOIs)

Most MAOIs work by blocking or inhibiting the enzyme monamine oxidase, which helps break down certain neurotransmitters in the brain. By inhibiting this enzyme, MOAIs increase levels of these neurotransmitters in the brain, which helps restore normal mood.

MAOIs like phenelzine (Nardil) and tranylcypromine (Parnate) have been used with some success in treating depressed adults. But many therapists are reluctant to use MAOIs with children and adolescents. The reason is that these medications can cause severe high blood pressure if the child taking them eats anything that contains an amino acid called tyramine, found in such foods as aged cheeses, sour cream, yogurt, chocolate, and beer. Since it's hard to keep kids on a restricted diet, most therapists prescribe MAOIs only when other medications have proven ineffective.

4. CHEMICALLY UNIQUE ANTIDEPRESSANTS

One of the most recent medications to attract the attention of doctors working with clinically depressed patients is venlafaxine (Effexor). This medication also works by inhibiting the reabsorption of serotonin and norepinephrine in the brain, but it is chemically unrelated to any other antidepressants. And because of its unique chemical structure, it also seems to cause fewer side effects.

Trazodone (Desyrel), nefazodone (Serzone), and bupropion (Wellbutrin) also have chemical structures unrelated to other antidepressants. Although the use of these medications in the treatment of adult depression is well established, experience with children is more limited.

5. LITHIUM

Lithium is a medication widely used to treat bipolar disorder, which, as discussed earlier, is also known as manic-depressive disorder. But it is also prescribed for patients with clinical depression (or unipolar disorder), even when the patient has shown no signs of manic behavior. Usually, however, lithium is recommended for children who have depression mixed with severe behavior problems, like frequent, uncontrollable temper tantrums, or for kids whose relatives have bipolar disorder that has been successfully treated with lithium. Physicians may also prescribe lithium for clinically depressed children who have not responded well to any other medication.

Although we don't know exactly how lithium works, its therapeutic effects are well established. But as with most medications, there are potential side effects, including nausea, vomiting, diarrhea, stomachaches, hand tremors, thirst and frequent urination, and fatigue, although they usually subside within a few days. Longer-term side effects occasionally include weight gain, changes in thyroid functioning, and kidney problems. As with all medication, your child should have a thorough medical exam and periodic checkups to make sure the lithium is not causing any significant or troublesome side effects.

■ Helping Your Child on Medication

While your child is on medication, there are many things you can do to help support the treatment and increase the likelihood that the medication will be effective. Here are a few simple, effective tips:

- *Learn all you can.* Be sure to ask your doctor or pharmacist for materials you can read, do some on-line research, or simply go to the library and check the latest annual edition of *Physician's Desk Reference* (popularly known as the *PDR*), which lists extensive information about medications. Understand, however, that for each medication it includes, the *PDR* lists all possible side effects—even extremely rare ones. Before you become alarmed by anything you read in the *PDR*, check with your doctor to see which side effects you need to worry about.

- *Ask questions.* If you don't fully understand why your child's doctor prescribes a particular medication, ask. In fact, when any medication is prescribed for your child, you should always raise a number of questions, such as:

level. The physician may also want to add something like "I want you to understand that you can't get addicted to antidepressants. They work by helping you feel better emotionally and physically."

Stick to the schedule. In order to help the antidepressant work most effectively, make sure your child takes his medication according to the prescribed schedule. If he misses a dose, don't try to make up for it by doubling the medication next time, unless your doctor advises it. Just resume the normal schedule and try to stick to it more carefully.

In reality, it can be hard for kids to remember to take their medications several times a day. Asking the doctor to prescribe a medication that can be taken once or twice a day should improve the likelihood that dosages won't be forgotten and skipped.

■ Take charge of all antidepressant medication. Antidepressants in general and tricyclics in particular can be extremely dangerous if taken in an overdose. So be sure that you or another responsible adult oversees how and when your child takes her medication. Even if your youngster is a teenager and you want to empower her by letting her take charge of her medication, it's generally not a good idea to hand over the whole bottle and say, "Take these three times a day." Remember, your child is taking medication because she is suffering from depression— so it's best to err on the side of safety. Unless your doctor recommends otherwise, dispense all medication yourself.

If your child needs to take a dose of medication during the school day, I suggest that you speak directly with the school nurse. You (and/or your child's physician) can usually make arrangements with her to hold the medication and to make sure that your child takes the proper dose at the right time. In working with the school, you'll probably discover that many of your child's classmates also take medication—and for a variety of reasons. So your child isn't likely to feel singled out or stigmatized.

■ Keep all appointments with your child's doctor. It's often helpful to bring a written list of questions you want to ask the doctor to ensure that you won't forget. If, however, important questions or concerns arise between appointments, don't hesitate to call the doctor. This is particularly true if the question is urgent; remember, most doctors

—Has this medication been used with children for a

—Why did you choose it?

—How is it different from other medications we mig

—What side effects should I expect?

—Which ones should I worry about?

—Is there anything I can do to minimize any negative

—How will I know if the medication is helping?

—How long will it take to work?

—How long will it take to know if it's not working?

—How will I know if my child is doing better?

—What changes in my child will I see first?

Finally, if the doctor prescribing the medication is no primary therapist, find out how these two clinicians will with each other.

■ *Talk with your child.* Together with the doctor, careful your child why he is taking medication and how the med affect him. Not only does this allow your youngster to hel own progress, but it also gives you and the physician th clear up any misconceptions your child may have. Ma instance, feel guilty and responsible for their depression ar taking medication as a punishment. Others may equate ta pressants with illicit drugs and worry they may get addicte

So with you present, the doctor will probably say someth to your young child: "You know how you've been feelin and tired lately? Well, it's important for you to understand feelings are not your fault; you're not being bad or lazy. Tl is that you have an illness called depression.

"There are lots of ways we help people with depression like talking about how you feel, including what's going o and at school. We also have special medicine that can help ents and I decided it would be a good idea for you to try i make your bad feelings go away overnight because it ta weeks to work. But pretty quickly it should help you sleep better, and have more energy."

Your doctor can use a similar explanation for your older chi ing the vocabulary to suit a youngster of his age and devel have arrangements by which you can reach them in an emergency. If for some reason the physician isn't available, however, you can call the emergency room of a local hospital or academic medical center.

■ *Ensure communication among all doctors and therapists treating your child.* Many children on medication will be involved with several clinicians, such as a pediatrician, a mental health therapist who is not a medical doctor, and a child psychiatrist. It's important for these professionals to communicate regularly with one another so that they are all aware of what medication the child is taking, which, if any, side effects have appeared, and changes in the child's physical or emotional condition.

When you are dealing with good doctors, such communication happens automatically, through correspondence, telephone calls, or face-to-face meetings. But check with your child's doctors periodically to make sure they are communicating with one another.

■ *Discuss with your child's doctor how much information is appropriate and helpful to share with the school.* Teachers and administrators may need to have some information about your child—for instance, it's important to let the school nurse know that your youngster is taking medication and to work with her if he needs to take a dosage during school hours. But you want to be cautious about how much detail you provide. Remember, school records do not always have the same promise of confidentiality that medical records do. Your child's doctor can help you determine just how much information you need to share.

More Intensive Treatments

Most depressed children respond quite well to a combination of individual therapy, family therapy, and medication. But for those few who do not, or for youngsters who are dangerous to themselves or others, more intensive programs are available and your child's therapist may refer you to one of them.

Today, many programs offer a full continuum of treatment services. For example, at Choate, the network of affiliated mental health programs where I work, we provide day treatment, home-based therapy, short-term crisis intervention, therapeutic foster care, residential treatment, and inpatient hospitalization.

■ **Day Treatment Programs**

Children involved with these programs are treated on an outpatient basis. Depending on the individual's needs, a child can participate in either half- or full-day programs from one to seven days a week. Some children attend their regular school and come to the day treatment program after classes are over. Others take classes at the program, working with a certified teacher.

Day treatment programs may include intensive, individualized therapy (several sessions a week) as well as group and family therapy. Children may also be involved in substance abuse prevention, anger management, and self-esteem-building programs, depending on the needs of the individual youngster.

■ **Home-Based Therapy**

In this program, trained therapists regularly visit the child and his family in their own home. Depending on the individual patient, treatment may include family therapy and helping parents develop ways to improve their child's behavior.

Sometimes, our home-based program is also used on an emergency basis to help stabilize a crisis, such as helping the family cope with a child's attempted suicide. In such cases, a treatment team, which is available twenty-four hours a day, seven days a week, goes to the family's home and stays as long as is necessary to help the parents develop a concrete plan to ensure the child's immediate safety.

Home-based therapy is a powerful intervention. It makes treatment immediate and very real for families since there is no separation between what goes on at home and what happens in treatment. Home-based therapy can be a potent tool in helping connect formal, therapeutic work with the everyday life of children and families.

Such emergency, home-based intervention really does work. At

Choate, we've found that an overwhelming majority of the family crises we encounter can be handled safely and effectively without having to remove the child from the home.

■ Short-Term Crisis Intervention

When children in crisis can't be safely helped at home—such as when a child repeatedly runs away or engages in dangerous or threatening behavior that requires around-the-clock treatment—they may need a brief period of treatment in an out-of-home setting. At Choate we have a program called STEP, which stands for Short-Term Emergency Placement. In a STEP program, children stay anywhere from one to seven days in a small, homelike setting that can accommodate four to six children. The program is staffed twenty-four hours a day by professionals specially trained to ensure each child's safety during a crisis period. STEP programs have been used effectively for children as young as five and as old as eighteen.

Children are also seen by child psychiatrists affiliated with the program and, whenever appropriate, by the child's individual therapist. The focus here is on rapid evaluation and stabilization, as opposed to long-term treatment.

■ Therapeutic Foster Care

In some communities, similar emergency placement programs function as part of the therapeutic foster care system. Therapeutic foster care can also provide longer-term care for troubled children who are having a hard time in their natural home either because of their own problems or because of ongoing family difficulties, such as drug use, alcoholism, or physical or sexual abuse.

Here's how it works. Typically, a social service agency recruits a couple as foster parents who agree to care for a troubled child in their own home. Ideally, these foster parents will have professional mental health or human service experience, as well the ability to provide their foster child with a structured, nurturing home life. A clinical team, which may include a social worker, psychologist, and child psychiatrist, works with the foster parents to help the child live successfully in this home. Twenty-four-hour staff support is also made available to the foster family in the event of a problem or crisis.

In addition, the clinical team works with the child's natural parents to help them learn more effective ways to manage their child in their own home. The foster parents, too, try to build a good working relationship with the natural parents, encouraging them to stay actively involved in their child's daily life. They also arrange for their foster child to make regular visits home. The goal of therapeutic foster care: to help both the foster child and his biological parents learn how to live together happily and safely.

■ Residential Treatment

This level of treatment can take place in a residential treatment center or school, or in a smaller, group-home setting. Children here typically receive psychiatric consultation and other treatment services. Children in residence either attend their own, regular school or one affiliated with the treatment center and, wherever possible, return home to their families for periodic visits.

The purpose of residential treatment, which may continue for several months to several years, is to provide children with an intensive, therapeutic setting designed to help them understand their feelings, change their behavior, and learn to improve their interactions with peers. These programs often help children who have had difficulty in other settings strengthen everyday living skills, including coping with stress, frustration, and disappointment. In this manner, residential treatment can serve as a springboard by which children can return to their families or prepare for a successful transition to a less intensive therapeutic setting.

■ Inpatient Hospitalization

The 1980s saw a dramatic increase in the development of hospital-based services for children, particularly adolescents. The last few years, however, have witnessed a dramatic reversal of this trend. In-patient hospitalization, which includes intensive, ongoing individual psychotherapy, group therapy, and such treatment techniques as art or music therapy, is now relatively rare. In general, it occurs only when no other safe alternatives are effective or when specialized diagnostic or medical evaluation is necessary. And even when children are hospitalized, stays that would have continued for many months now last for only about a week.

In large part, this trend toward shorter stays is driven by third-party reimbursement programs. Previously, insurance policies covered only in- or outpatient treatment. As a result, many children who could not be treated as outpatients were hospitalized even when less intensive treatment settings might have been equally or more effective. Today, though, reimbursement is available for less-intensive programs. Hospitals—with their larger staffs, wider range of evaluation and treatment techniques, medical support services, and safety precautions—are used mostly for initial evaluation and stabilization of those children of any age—even as young as four or five—who cannot be safely assessed in other settings, such as a short-term crisis intervention program. Most of the actual treatment, however, generally occurs in less intensive programs.

■ Questions to Ask If Your Therapist Recommends Out-of-Home Treatment

Even though you trust your child's doctor and have faith in her recommendations, allowing your youngster to be placed in any out-of-home treatment setting is a very painful decision. And it is not one that can—or should—be made lightly. In fact, I strongly recommend that before you agree to any such placement, you ask your child's therapist the following questions (adapted from the "Facts for Families" series, produced by the American Academy of Child and Adolescent Psychiatry):

1. Why is this type of treatment necessary?
2. How will it help my child?
3. What does the treatment program include?
4. How many professionals will be treating my child? Do they work together as a team?
5. How long will my child be away from home?

6. Is this facility or hospital accredited by the Joint Commission on the Accreditation of Healthcare Organizations (JCAHO) as a treatment facility for children of my child's age?

7. What will the treatment cost? Is it covered by insurance? When is payment expected?

8. Will my child be in a special unit for children?

9. What will happen if my child needs to stay longer than expected and I can no longer afford to pay?

10. How will I (and other members of my family) be involved in the treatment? How often can I visit my child?

11. Will I be consulted regarding discharge?

12. What will happen to my child after discharge? What will the after-care treatment be?

Before you agree to place your child in an out-of-home setting, try to visit the setting yourself and talk with the staff so that you make sure you understand and feel comfortable with their methods and treatment philosophy. And if you have any doubts about the appropriateness of the care for your child, get a second opinion from another therapist.

■ Your Role in Intensive/Out-of-Home Therapy

Today, most intensive programs involve parents in many aspects of the treatment process. In addition to individual sessions with your family—often including siblings and other very close relatives, like a grandparent or aunt who may be living with you—some programs hold meetings with several families at once. These "multifamily" sessions are a powerful tool in helping you and your child learn from the experiences of others. Most families find it comforting to know that they are not the only ones struggling with the issues surrounding depression.

Often, parents will also meet separately with their child's psychiatrist, primary therapist, or case manager, the professional responsible for coordinating all the aspects of your child's treatment. In these sessions, staff explain the results of any evaluations and share their opinions and recommendations regarding your child's treatment. It also offers a good opportunity for parents to raise any issues or ask questions about their child's treatment.

■ Know Your Rights

Let me make two final points about more intensive modes of therapy, particularly out-of-home treatment. First, don't let yourself get intimidated by your child's doctors or by any of the hospital staff. If you don't agree with their recommendations, you have the right to say no. Your child's well-intentioned therapist will render his best professional judgments, but it's up to you, the parent, to make the final decision. And as I have said before, if you're in doubt, do not hesitate to get another opinion.

Second, seek the least intensive, shortest mode of treatment that you and the therapist feel will help your child. Even though long-term treatment can have many beneficial effects, I worry about young kids getting stuck in the process and having therapy become the main focus of their lives. If a child stays in treatment too long, it can begin to interfere with all those normal experiences of childhood—playing with friends, taking music lessons, going on school trips—that are so important to normal growth and development. In my mind, the goal of therapy isn't necessarily to fix all problems; instead, the objective is to deal with the issues, conflicts, or symptoms that are disrupting a child's life. Your goal as a parent—and the aim of any good therapist— is to help relieve your child's suffering as fast as possible so that he can return to his main job: being a kid—and, eventually, becoming a healthy, happy, resilient adult.

Chapter

9

Parents as Partners:

What You Can Do to Help Your Depressed Child

Last year I was feeling totally bummed. I didn't want to talk to anyone. I just wanted everybody to leave me alone, especially my parents. But now that I feel better, I think knowing that my mom and dad loved me really helped me get through it.

—Andrea, age fifteen

As a parent of a depressed child, you now know you can play a significant role in helping your youngster overcome her illness by finding a skilled therapist and working with him to develop and support an appropriate treatment plan. But you probably still have many questions: Should I treat my child with extra caution, trying hard not to upset her? Or will being too careful just make things worse? Should I ask her questions about her therapy sessions? Or should I avoid the subject so as not to make her uncomfortable? Other than taking her to her therapy appointments, what can I do to ensure her progress, to help her get better faster?

As you read this chapter, you'll find the answers to all these questions. But keep one guiding principle in mind: *Effective treatment of children with depression depends on establishing a strong, three-way partnership among you, your child, and the therapist.* There needs to be open communication, an honest exchange of information and, above all, trust. This is why, whenever I work with depressed youngsters— from preschoolers to adolescents—I welcome and encourage parents' input and support. In fact, I really *need* them if I am to do my job as well as possible. So let's take some time to explore the many things parents can do to become active partners in helping their depressed child.

How to Work Best with Your Child's Therapist

■ Become an Accurate Observer

Since therapists usually see their young patients only in session, they need the parents to be their extra eyes and ears, keeping tabs on how the children are doing at home, in social situations, and, when possible, at school. You might find it helpful to keep a notebook handy to jot down any changes you observe so that you can share the information with the therapist. In it you might note that instead of waking up frequently and wanting to crawl into your bed, for the past two weeks your six-year-old has been sleeping peacefully through the night. Or you might report that you've seen a real decrease (or increase) in the number of fights between your depressed eight-year-old and her little brother.

If your child is taking antidepressant medication, you may want to take note of any reactions or side effects he may be having, such as stomachaches, rashes, drowsiness, or difficulty concentrating. Report them to the therapist and the doctor who prescribed the medication (if different from your child's therapist) as soon as possible.

By the way, you don't always have to supply all this information yourself. You can encourage your child to share some significant news with his doctor. For instance, you might say, "You know, I think Dr. Fassler would be interested in knowing how you're doing in school. Why don't you bring your last report card with you when you meet with him next week?"

■ If You're Not Sure What the Therapist Wants to Know, Ask

As we've already discussed, therapists are individuals with different styles and approaches to treatment. Some are especially attuned to your child's relationships with family members; others are more concerned with changes in your child's behavior, or in his interactions with other kids. If your child's therapist has not spelled out the kinds of information he would find most helpful, by all means ask.

■ Respect Your Child's Right to Privacy

If you've ever been in therapy yourself, you know how important it is to feel confident that whatever you discuss in your sessions will stay between you and your therapist. Well, your child feels the same way.

Children in treatment are entitled to the same right of privacy as adults. In fact, kids will feel relaxed enough to open up to their therapist *only* if they are secure in the knowledge that what they say will remain confidential.

Every therapist may have a different approach, but whenever I begin treating a depressed child—no matter what the youngster's age—I lay out the ground rules. I explain that whatever she tells me will stay private—with one important exception: if something she says makes me concerned for her safety, I'll let her parents know. A child who tells me that she's been cutting her arms and legs because she feels "like I'm not worth anything" or a youngster who reveals that she is thinking about running away from home knows that this is the kind of information I will share with her mom and dad. But even then, I talk to my young patient beforehand, saying something like "This is one of those things I need to talk to your mom and dad about." This approach rarely puts children off; in fact, most of my patients find it comforting to know that I will do whatever I need to do to keep them safe.

Parents, too, need to respect a child's right to privacy and avoid grilling him about what goes on in therapy. On the other hand, you should expect that a good therapist will keep you apprised of your child's progress, at least in general terms. When I work with young children, I usually see the child privately for about forty to fifty minutes, and then bring in the parent (or parents) for another five to fifteen minutes during which the three of us (therapist, parent, and child) can discuss the youngster's progress, share observations and concerns, and ask questions.

These "family meetings" are not formal therapy sessions; we are not zeroing in on specific family issues and dynamics. Instead, these brief conferences are simply an opportunity for an open exchange of information and ideas. During an end-of-session conference with Johnny's parents, I might say, "Johnny and I talked about what we would share with you today, and we both want you to know that our sessions seem to be going well. Johnny is doing some pretty hard work expressing some very difficult thoughts and feelings. Through playing games and drawing, we've been exploring themes of anger and sadness, and I think we're starting to understand more about what's behind some of the problems Johnny's been having at home. I'm wondering if you've been noticing any changes recently, either good or bad, or if there are any particular issues you think we should all talk about together?"

My approach with adolescents differs only in that I usually have less direct contact with their moms and dads. I work alone with the teenager during most sessions, and meet with the parent(s) and youngster together about once a month. But even when working with teenagers, I try to give parents a sense of how the therapy is progressing without disturbing the therapeutic relationship I have established with their child. I never want my patients to worry "What is my doctor telling my parents (or vice versa) when I'm not around? What's going on behind my back?"

If Mom and Dad insist on speaking with me privately because they don't feel comfortable sharing some information while their child is present, I will certainly meet with them. But I will let my patient know about the meeting and work with the parents to find the best way to discuss whatever they tell me with their child.

■ Don't Try to Build a Secret Alliance with Your Child's Therapist

In order to give therapy its best chance for success, therapists try to develop a solid, trusting relationship with their young patients. This is why I rarely speak with parents without their child being present, and why I generally refer parents in need of couples or family therapy to another clinician. I don't want to create any secret alliances between the child's parents or other relatives and myself.

I also don't want my work with the child to be overly influenced by what I hear about him from other people. Being able to see the world through my patient's eyes is extremely important to me. If I know something that he doesn't know, it compromises my ability to view his life circumstances from his perspective, which could make my work with the child less effective.

Additionally, I believe therapy works best when my patient decides what we discuss in our session. But if I know some piece of important information that the child does not—say, for example, that a much-loved uncle is not just ill but dying—I might be tempted to ask the youngster how he feels about that even though it may not be something he wants to talk about. As a result, I, rather than my patient, wind up determining the direction of our discussions—a situation that can decrease the effectiveness of therapy.

■ Stick to the Schedule

Try to make sure that your child keeps each of his appointments with the therapist, and try to avoid veering from the schedule. Predictability and consistency are important—and therapeutic—to a child with depression.

■ Avoid Using Your Child's Therapist as Your Own

Occasionally, a parent who is very needy or lonely tries to spend a great deal of the child's therapy session talking to me, either about her depressed youngster or her own problems. When this happens, I try to explain that establishing a separate relationship with me may interfere with the special bond that her child and I have developed, and that this is an alliance she needs to respect and preserve.

If you find yourself wanting to spend more and more time talking to your child's doctor, consider finding your own therapist with whom you can share your feelings and concerns. That way, you can respect the relationship between your child and his therapist while still getting the support you need. (In fact, you can ask your child's therapist for a referral to a clinician who specializes in working with adults.)

■ Present a United Front

It's important that *both* parents support their child's treatment plan. Ongoing arguments between Mom and Dad about whether or not their child should be in therapy can undermine the treatment and make it harder for the youngster to get well. If one parent is always putting down therapy, the child may start to feel ambivalent or negative about treatment—particularly if he closely identifies with the dissenting parent or has a strong desire to please him or her.

Parents' attitudes can have another effect. If Mom or Dad doubts the potential benefit of the treatment, for example, the child can sense this and may periodically "forget" to take his antidepressant medication. Too many missed doses will reduce the medication's effectiveness. Additionally, a parent who is ambivalent about treatment may over-react to relatively minor side effects, like dry mouth or constipation, using them as an excuse to stop the medication prematurely, which also could hinder the child's progress.

On the flip side, however, parents' unified, accepting attitude toward medication is more likely to contribute to the treatment's success. The bottom line: You and your spouse need to get in sync about treatment so that you can offer consistent, unconflicted, ongoing support to your depressed youngster.

■ Give Therapy Time

Don't expect therapy to make your child better immediately. In fact, some kids' behavior may actually worsen for a while, particularly during the first few weeks of treatment. One reason for this is that when children are depressed they may not have the energy to act out. But as their depression begins to lift, they feel more energetic and may begin to display behavior problems that were masked by their previous lethargy.

Additionally, many depressed children have stored a great deal of anger inside. As they deal with this anger in treatment, their feelings often erupt into problem behaviors, particularly if they were quiet and withdrawn before they began therapy. This is why the depressed child who used to sit alone on the sidelines while the other kids played may suddenly get involved in schoolyard fights as he begins to wrestle with his inner thoughts and feelings in treatment.

Although a significant part of the therapeutic process, these kinds of negative changes can be very upsetting to parents and teachers. They certainly were to a thirty-seven-year-old dad named Jeff. His son, Ricky, was only twelve years old when many months of lethargy and sadness led to a dramatic suicide attempt: One morning, Ricky set himself on fire.

"It was an awful moment, one I really don't like to think about," Jeff recalls. "It was only through the grace of God that we found him quickly and got the fire out so that his burns were relatively minor. After that, we got him into treatment with a child psychiatrist." But those first few months were tough.

"I could tell when his mood was about to change," says Jeff. "He'd start getting disrespectful toward me and my wife. He'd become very belligerent. A few times, he even took a swing at me."

After several months, however, Ricky's depression began to improve and his behavior became much less confrontational. As Jeff learned, sometimes you just have to be patient and not get discouraged and to understand that these outbursts are quite useful to the child; when they are discussed in therapy, they often provide grist for the therapeutic mill. What's more, these changes tend to be temporary. As your child continues to deal with his depression in therapy, not only will they disappear but his overall behavior will improve substantially. Although each child and situation is different, in most cases families start to see improvement within the first four to six weeks of treatment; full recovery, however, generally requires several months.

Beyond Therapy: How to Help Your Child Yourself

Effective parenting skills are always important, but when your child is depressed, they're critical. At most, your child is working with a therapist one or two hours a week—which means that the majority of the time, you're on your own. Helping him overcome his depression will take more than good, commonsense parenting; it will take a clear understanding of—and a determination to practice—these specific tactics and suggestions.

■ Show Your Love and Affection

When adults get depressed, they often feel unloved and unlovable. Children are no different. And since you are their main source of love and support, they need your hugs and smiles, and your praise for their good qualities, skills, and accomplishments. Of course, the way you demonstrate your affection will depend on your child's temperament and age; after all, most sixteen-year-olds will not tolerate too many hugs from Mom or Dad—and *certainly* not in public! Just be sure to show your child, as often as possible, how much you care.

■ Strive for Normality

Many times, parents of a depressed child feel they need to walk on eggshells around their youngster. As a result, normal family interactions, rules, and routines often break down. While your child *is* in a more fragile emotional state these days—and there's a natural and understandable tendency to let things slide a bit—it's best to treat him as normally as you can.

For example, continue to hold family celebrations. But be sure to take your cues from your child as to what kind of festivities he might enjoy. Right now he may feel more comfortable with toned-down events, like having one or two friends over for a birthday lunch at home rather than inviting fifteen boisterous kids to a party at a huge amusement park.

It's also wise not to let depression lead to a total collapse of family rules and routines. If the rule in your home is no TV until all homework is finished, stick to that policy. If your child is supposed to help set the table for dinner, he should continue to do so.

Sharon is the twenty-nine-year-old mother of ten-year-old Hannah, who was diagnosed with depression two years ago. She believes "letting Hannah be normal" is one of the important things she does to help her daughter. "When my child was first diagnosed," says Sharon, "all she wanted to do was sleep. I let this go on for a while, but then, after talking with her doctor, I realized I had to stop treating her as if she were different. So I started insisting that she get up every morning, get dressed, and do her chores, like picking up her room and helping her seven-year-old sister make the beds. And every evening after dinner, she had to clear the table. Whenever my husband and I would go out and get a baby-sitter for the kids—Hannah is the oldest of four—we told her that it was her job to help the baby-sitter take care of the 'little kids,' which made her feel important.

"For a while," Sharon continues, "she fussed about having chores and responsibilities. But now I think she likes it because it makes her feel better about herself."

Keep in mind, however, that occasionally a depressed child or teenager may not have the physical energy to do certain rigorous chores, like washing the car or shoveling snow out of the driveway. In that case, try to be flexible enough to assign her a less taxing chore, like watering the plants or feeding the cat. The point is to make sure that your depressed child isn't excluded or excused from normal family responsibilities, while understanding that your youngster may not be able to do all she did before.

■ Keep Talking—and Listening

Don't be afraid to engage your child not only in everyday conversations—"How was school today?" "Did you play basketball with your friends at recess?"—but also in discussions that give him the chance to express his feelings and concerns. Just don't push. If you notice that your child is especially mopey one day, it's fine to say "What's up?" But if he doesn't feel like talking just then, that's okay, too. Just let him know that you're interested and available whenever he's ready.

Be aware, though, that therapy often stirs up a lot of issues in a child, some of which you may not be very comfortable discussing. For instance, although you got divorced three years ago, have established an amicable relationship with your ex-spouse, and have even moved on to a new romance, your thirteen-year-old may now start asking questions like "Why did you and Dad get divorced? Was he having an affair?" or "How come we had to move to a new house after Mom left?" So be prepared to answer honestly and calmly any questions your child might have in a manner appropriate to her age and developmental level.

Sometimes the most important thing you can do to help your child is simply to listen. Adrienne, forty, whose ten-year-old daughter still struggles with depression, finds this a valuable lesson. "I had to learn to listen better. Before, I was always interrupting her with comments or questions, or doing something else, like fixing dinner or watching TV when she was trying to talk. Now I stop what I'm doing and really listen. Sometimes, when she's very out of sorts, I don't even make a comment. I just wait till she's gotten everything off her chest. Then I'll either say something or wait a day or two and come back to it. And it's made a big difference. She knows she can talk to me about anything and that she can always have my full attention when she really needs it."

- **Encourage Your Child's Continuing Development**
  There's a tendency on the part of some depressed children to stop participating in activities, avoid socializing with friends, quit doing homework, and start spending an unusual amount of time alone spacing out in front of the TV, listening to music, or sleeping. But too much inactivity isn't helpful to your child and should not be encouraged; instead, foster his active participation in a variety of enjoyable pastimes.

Of course, you don't want to overwhelm your youngster. A depressed child can actually find it painful to participate in certain activities, and pushing him too hard can exacerbate his depression. Your son may be feeling too vulnerable to risk the potential rejection involved in auditioning for the school play; it may make him feel even more worthless and sad than he already does. But he can join the stage crew, even if that means he'll miss his afternoon bus for a couple of weeks and you'll either have to pick him up or have to arrange for someone else to help with transportation.

Another example: Your depressed daughter is feeling too insecure to enjoy a month-long tour of some national parks with her scout troop.

If she goes only to please you and spends her time there alone, sad, and isolated, this may further damage her fragile self-esteem. But it's probably not too much to sign her up for a twice-a-week summer gymnastics or art class, even if that means spending a good deal of time scouting out an appropriate program.

Children's ability to grow and develop doesn't stop because they are depressed. So be sure to encourage and support their participation in age-appropriate activities and events.

■ Help Your Child Have Fun

Depressed children still have things they like to do. Focusing on these activities and facilitating your child's participation in them will help your youngster avoid becoming overly absorbed in his depression and treatment.

As the parents of one depressed fifteen-year-old commented, "When our son seems particularly sad, we take him to a hockey game. He loves hockey, so it's hard for him to stay really down when we're at the stadium. If there's no game on, we go hiking. Not only does it cheer him up, but spending time together as a family seems to help us all communicate. He's more likely to tell us what's on his mind when we're doing fun things together."

■ Help Free Your Child of Negative-Thinking Traps

As we've already discussed, lots of depressed children get trapped into cycles of hopelessness and negative thinking. They get a bad grade in math and say to themselves, "I'll *never* get any better. I just don't understand numbers, and I *never* will. I'm too dumb." Or they begin classes at a new school and if they don't make friends the first day, they say to themselves, "*Nobody* ever likes me. I'll *never* have any friends." Such thought and belief patterns are excruciatingly painful to children and serve to perpetuate their depression. But there are a number of things you can do to help.

One is to acknowledge your depressed child's feelings without necessarily accepting his conclusions. You could say something like, "I know that you feel like you have no friends and that nobody likes you, and that that's a pretty bad feeling. There were times when I was growing up when I felt the same way. But I also know that you're a great kid and you're good at a lot of things. And I think that when you start feeling better, it will be easier for you to make friends. And don't forget that no matter what, I'm always your friend."

Another way to counteract your child's pessimistic thinking is to offer a more balanced perspective. If your eight-year-old didn't get invited to a classmate's birthday party and she believes "nobody" likes her, you could say, "I know you feel disappointed and hurt about Jamie's party. But remember that you went to two birthday parties last weekend, and you just got an invitation to Cindy's party for next weekend. I think you really have *lots* of friends even though it may not feel like it right now."

One important note: While you can help free your child from the trap of negative thinking, it's not your job to be your child's therapist. You are not responsible for uncovering the roots of your child's problem, for making a diagnosis, or for prescribing treatment. You can leave that to your child's therapist and spend your energy concentrating on giving your child all the love and support he needs.

▪ Respect Your Child's Feelings

Depressed children experience many intense emotions. This can be difficult for parents because it hurts to see the child you love feeling sad, discouraged, pessimistic, or even suicidal. Your natural tendency is to try to cheer your youngster up. But in doing so, you run the risk of trivializing your depressed child's feelings, which only makes him feel humiliated and devalued and keeps you at an emotional distance.

A much better tactic is to acknowledge and respect your child's emotions. In this way, you convey the message that you take your youngster seriously, that his feelings are important, and that you're not afraid of any thoughts or emotions he might have.

Carl, forty-one, the father of a depressed fourteen-year-old named Robin, works hard at accepting his daughter's feelings. "I try never to criticize the way Robin thinks about things or to make light of her problems. She recently had a boyfriend for the first time, but things haven't worked out for them and they're in the process of breaking up. My first reaction was to say, 'Oh, this is no big deal; it happens to everybody. At your age, it's easy.' But that's not fair to her. The fact is it *isn't* easy, especially not for Robin. Right now it's her whole world, and she's in a great deal of pain. So what I said instead was, 'This must be really hard for you. Is there anything your mom or I can do to help? I want you to know that we'll always be there for you when you need us.' "

■ Help Your Child to Relax

Many depressed children never learned how to relax and comfort themselves. If that's true of your child, help her discover activities and techniques that soothe and calm her. Start by telling your child the things you do to relax, like taking a hot bath or going for a long walk. Then ask her to think about things she likes to do—drawing a picture, reading a favorite story or book, or shooting baskets out in the back-yard—and encourage her to do these things when she's feeling tense or anxious.

■ Reduce as Much Home-Based Stress as Possible

Back in chapter 2, we talked about how family tensions can heighten your child's risk for depression. Well, if your child is already depressed, such home-based stress can exacerbate his problems and slow the progress of therapy. It's helpful, then, to make a concerted effort to keep home tensions and disruptions to a minimum. Here are some suggestions as to how.

- Try to maintain certain regular routines. Depressed children find a reliable schedule reassuring.
- Don't turn family life into around-the-clock therapy. Not every event, occurrence, or action has to be viewed through the lens of your child's depression. If he breaks a drinking glass, it's not nec-essarily an act of hostility; it may simply be an accident. If he turns down a friend's invitation to a movie, it may be because he doesn't want to see that film, not because he's tired or with-drawing.
- Steer clear of major disruptions to your household. This is not a good time to move, change your child's school, or invite the in-laws over for a few weeks.

If, despite your best efforts, there continues to be a high degree of tension in your home, you may need some extra help. For instance, if you and your spouse can't seem to stop bickering, you could try seeing a therapist who specializes in couples counseling. If problems consistently arise between you and your children or among the kids themselves, family therapy may be helpful. Whatever the case, discuss the situation with your child's therapist. He or she can refer you to an appropriate and qualified clinician.

■ Help Your Child Protect His Privacy

Your child's therapy is a private matter that involves your youngster, his immediate family, and his therapist. Neither you nor your child should feel obligated to discuss the details of his treatment with other relatives and friends.

Still, many parents worry that "everyone will know" that their child is in therapy and that, as a result, he will be stigmatized by it. But in my experience, it is not therapy or treatment that stigmatizes a depressed child, but issues related to their behavior, such as acting out in class or problems with peers. That said, however, it is possible that someone may tease your child for being in therapy or for "seeing a shrink." If that happens, try to be as understanding and supportive as possible. You might say something like this to your child: "I know it hurts when people tease you, but they do it because they don't really understand how sad you've been feeling and how therapy can help you feel better."

■ Don't Make Depression a Family Secret

Although I view therapy as a private issue, at the same time I do not believe it should become a family secret. Insisting that no one in your family ever talk about your child's depression puts added pressure on your youngster by making her feel she has a secret she has to hide. It can even make her feel ashamed of her illness and treatment, and perpetuate her problems. At the same time, you want to make it clear that it's not necessary to tell everybody about her problems or her treatment because many people don't understand depression or what's involved in helping a depressed child.

But I've found that letting family members you love and trust know about your child's depression can be helpful. For one thing, telling close relatives that your youngster is depressed may help you discover whether other family members have ever suffered from similar problems. And, as we've said before, family and close friends can provide comfort and support for both you and your child.

On the other hand, if friends and relatives begin offering unsolicited advice and opinions and questioning your decisions, you don't have to defend your actions or share any details. There is absolutely nothing wrong with setting appropriate limits and boundaries for yourself and your child.

Suppose, for example, that your sister-in-law calls to say "I heard that Tara is so depressed that she's seeing a psychiatrist. That seems so drastic!" It is perfectly fine to respond with "I appreciate your concern, but I have confidence in Tara's therapist. I think we have things under control and are heading in the right direction."

One more word of advice: Keep the faith. Depression is a very serious illness—sometimes, even a lethal one. But it is also highly treatable, particularly when detected early. So don't give up. Remember that most children with depression respond well and quickly to treatment. By following the suggestions I've outlined in this chapter, you'll be doing a great deal to support your child and become an active partner in his recovery.

Chapter

10

How to Prevent Depression in Your Child:

Parenting for Resiliency

Preventing mental illness is a controversial issue. Some experts believe that major disorders like clinical depression are strictly genetic or neurobiological problems that cannot be prevented. Others, like myself, are convinced that while biological factors may predispose certain children and adults to depression, emotional and social events and considerations strongly influence whether or not depression actually develops.

However, current research using such radiographic tools as magnetic resonance imaging (MRI) and positron emission tomography (PET) is beginning to suggest that these two schools of thought may not be so different after all. It appears that stressful events may actually change brain chemistry and metabolism—which may help explain why certain circumstances and events increase a child's risk for depression.

Of course, all children experience some stressful situations, transitions, and losses while growing up. Most of these are fairly common, like moving to a new neighborhood, losing a school election, or breaking up with that first girlfriend or boyfriend. Others are more extraordinary, like experiencing the death of a parent or suffering the loss of their school or home in a devastating natural disaster. Yet both kinds of stressors can contribute to childhood depression.

Still, there's good news about bad events: They can be opportunities to guide your children along a healthy emotional path. Confronting stressful events gives children the opportunity to master effective and enduring coping skills that can help prevent depression—*even when youngsters are biologically or genetically predisposed to the disorder.* By learning and practicing the six techniques of parenting for resiliency— tactics *every* parent can use with *any* child—you can dramatically reduce a child's risk for depression both now and in the future. And you can influence the intensity, course, and outcome of depression when and if it does occur.

Parenting for Resiliency

The single most important thing you can do to protect your children from depression is to raise them to be resilient. By definition, resilient children are able to recover readily from disappointments, frustrations, or other misfortunes. They are much less likely to be overwhelmed by life's problems and challenges and, therefore, much less susceptible to depression.

When you parent for resiliency, you become the mediator, shaper, and interpreter of your children's experiences. By responding to your kids in positive, affirming ways you help them create the foundation for a flexible and dynamic coping style that will let them bounce back from life's dilemmas and move on happily and productively.

Preventative parenting for resiliency centers on six essential principles:

1. Loving and supporting the "real" child
2. Establishing predictability, availability, and security
3. Fostering open and honest communication
4. Adopting a constructive and balanced approach to discipline
5. Allowing children to experience life
6. Enhancing self-esteem

■ **Principle #1: Loving and Supporting the "Real" Child**

The birth of a new baby thrills every parent. As Mom and Dad gaze down at the infant, they can't help but imagine that their child will become the healthiest, happiest, smartest, and most successful individual in the entire world. But as that child begins to grow and develop, parents need to concentrate less on the idealized image—that is, who and what they would *like* their youngster to be—and more on understanding, loving, and supporting the unique person he *really is.*

Such understanding begins almost from the moment of birth. Does your newborn sleep soundly or awaken frequently? Will your toddler try a new breakfast food, or does he insist on eating the same cereal every morning? Is your preschooler happier climbing on the jungle gym or quietly putting together a jigsaw puzzle? What comforts your nine-year-old when he gets upset—music, cuddling, tossing a football around with his dad? And what irritates him? Is your teenager always surrounded by an energetic group of kids, or does she prefer the company of a single, close friend?

The better you know your child, the better you'll be able to help him develop an adaptive, resilient coping style that builds on his strengths—not his weaknesses—and enables him to achieve his wishes, goals, and dreams.

Sound like a big job? It is—but it's certainly not an impossible one. Here are some suggestions.

SHAPE THE SITUATION

Children who are continually placed in circumstances in which they *are* overwhelmed will eventually begin to *feel* overwhelmed. This overpowering sense of helplessness provides fertile ground for poor self-esteem and, ultimately, for the development of clinical depression. But if you understand your children and help set up experiences that support their strengths (as well as acknowledge their weaknesses), you can help build their emotional resiliency and keep them from feeling overwhelmed and depressed.

For instance, if your youngster is a terrific artist but completely tone deaf, don't force him to continue taking those hated trumpet lessons in school. Instead, acknowledge his lack of musical ability and encourage him to try an art class at the local museum or community center. If your teenager is a solid C student, don't insist that he apply to the most competitive colleges; you're only setting him up for failure and yourself for disappointment. Rather, encourage him to apply to good schools that will more likely welcome his abilities and strengths.

Here's an example that further illustrates how to shape a situation to fit your child. Seven-year-old Aaron was very shy and a bit unsure of his athletic skills. His mom, wanting to encourage her son to be more socially and physically active, thought that enrolling him in an after-school gymnastics class might be a good idea. But because she knew that her son might feel overwhelmed being in a new class with a group of kids he didn't know, she urged him to find a friend interested in joining him and offered to coordinate transportation to and from the gym. The result? Aaron had a great time, became quite good at gymnastics, and grew more confident in both his social and athletic skills.

Aaron's mom did all the right things. First, she paid attention to who her son really was—a bright, sweet, but somewhat shy and gawky youngster. Second, because she understood his vulnerabilities so well, she was able to help buffer him against any unnecessary discomfort by encouraging him to find a friend to take the class with him. Her approach helped construct a situation that enabled Aaron to feel good and succeed rather than to feel overpowered and defeated.

GO WITH THE GRAIN, NOT AGAINST IT

Raising a resilient child means going with the grain of her temperament and personality. By ensuring that your child feels comfortable enough to remain flexible and open to new ideas and experiences—rather than becoming closed off and rigid—you can help her reach her goals without feeling overwhelmed and depressed.

Last spring, for example, eight-year-old Lori told her parents that "everyone" in her class was going to overnight camp that summer and she wanted to go, too. Her parents' initial reaction was to say no because they knew that Lori became very anxious and rigid in new situations—especially if it meant being separated from her family. But since they respected their daughter and wanted to support her, they suggested that they visit the camp before enrolling her. That way, Lori could explore the situation in a way that was comfortable for her—

with the support and presence of her family and without any pressure to perform.

So one Saturday in early May, the family packed a picnic lunch, drove out to the camp, and toured the grounds. Lori saw where the lake was, where the recreation center was located, and where her cabin would be. Then they spread their blanket on the softball field, had lunch, and talked. Lori immediately expressed some reservations. She said she hadn't realized the camp was so big and was feeling increasingly anxious about sleeping away from home for "a whole month." But she felt conflicted because although she didn't want to go to this camp, she also didn't want to be the only kid in her class who stayed home all summer.

So Lori's parents suggested she consider day camp and, a few weeks later, took her to see one not far from their home. As soon as she explored the grounds, visited the stables, and met the camp director, she decided she'd like to try it, especially since she could come home every night. Her parents signed her up without hesitation. Although she was nervous before the big first day, Lori adjusted quickly. In fact, she enjoyed the experience so much that she couldn't wait to do it all over again the following summer. By going with Lori's natural tendencies—rather than against them—her parents provided their child with a positive experience that served to build, not damage, her emotional resilience.

ENCOURAGE SELF-AWARENESS

Lori's parents also taught her this important lesson: When you understand yourself and respect who you are, you can reach your goals more effectively and successfully. By taking Lori to visit the overnight camp and encouraging her to express her thoughts and feelings without judging or pushing her, Lori's parents helped her *discover for herself* that she was not yet ready to be apart from them for an extended period of time—and that that was perfectly okay. She could still enjoy the experience of summer camp by finding (with her parents' help) an alternative that was more appropriate to her wants and needs. Not only did Lori's parents respect their child, but they also taught her to understand and respect herself.

- **Principle #2: Establishing Predictability, Availability, and Security**

In order to grow up to be emotionally healthy, competent adults, children first need to reach out and explore the world around them. But they will do this only if they have a loving, secure, predictable home base from which to start.

Babies, for example, will be more likely to leave Mom's arms to investigate a new toy if they are sure that she (or another primary caregiver) will be there when they return. It's not much different for five- or six-year-olds going off to their first day of school; they'll find it a lot easier to say good-bye and enjoy this new experience if they know that a loving parent or caregiver will be waiting for them at day's end.

As they grow older, children raised in a loving, predictable home begin to make this sense of security a part of themselves. They develop a sense of self-confidence that allows them to explore and experience the world around them and to confront life's difficulties and frustrations without becoming overwhelmed and depressed.

How can you create such a secure, strong foundation for your youngster? Here are some concrete suggestions.

CREATE A DEPENDABLE, SUPPORTIVE EMOTIONAL ENVIRONMENT

Children need to know that their parents' responses are predictable. It's easy to understand just how important this is by listening to adult children of alcoholics recount their rather extreme experiences. One hallmark of their childhood is that they never knew which parent—a calm, sober dad or a tense, angry one; a loving, attentive mom or a distant, self-absorbed one—they would find when they walked into their home. So often they grew up feeling insecure and unable to trust, which heightened their risk for depression.

Responding to your children in an emotionally predictable, loving, and supportive way—demonstrating again and again that they can count on you to react consistently—will help your youngsters feel safe and secure.

SPEND TIME ALONE WITH YOUR CHILD ON A FREQUENT, DEPENDABLE BASIS

In earlier chapters, we've discussed the importance of setting up predictable routines and rituals in your home. But there's something else you can do to establish a secure foundation: Spend lots of time alone with your child, and do it on a dependable basis. In fact, giving your child lots of predictable opportunities to be with you is more important than what you actually do during that time or how long you spend doing it.

When your child knows that she can count on watching TV with you a few evenings a week, or that she will get to run errands with you on weekends, or even that she can accompany you on your weekly trip to the supermarket, she develops a stronger sense of security and constancy. She knows that she has regular opportunities to discuss a problem she may be having, or to express any feelings she may be experiencing—or simply to enjoy your company.

One of my patients, a slightly chubby twelve-year-old named Nathan, knew that his dad, a lawyer who had played college baseball, usually picked him up after school at least once a week to go for a long drive together. So Nathan picked that time to tell his father something important: that he didn't want to go to baseball camp. "I just shut my eyes tight, took a deep breath, and said, 'Dad, I really don't want to go to camp this year. I know it's the same camp you went to and that you really liked it, but I don't.'

"I was really nervous about telling him," Nathan confided in me, "so what I did before was to picture where we'd be—in the car—and then practice what I'd say. When I actually told him, my dad was a little upset, but he was okay with it. And the best part is I don't have to go to camp!" Clearly, knowing in advance that he would have a time and place to broach a difficult issue with his father helped Nathan voice his wishes. And the reliability of this father-son time let Nathan know that his dad loved and valued him.

ESTABLISH CLEAR, RELIABLE GUIDELINES

It's confusing and disconcerting to a child when he doesn't know where he stands—which is why you need to set up reasonable, consistent, and predictable guidelines in your home. You can teach your children guidelines in two ways: one, by creating clear rules, and two, by being a good role model.

When establishing a rule, let your child know why you created it. For instance, you don't run with sticks in your hand because you could fall and get hurt; you can't watch TV until all your homework is done because if you do, you may be too tired to concentrate later. That way, your child can understand that rules are made for a reason.

Enforcing the rules consistently also helps kids get the approval they want and need. They know that if they follow the guidelines they'll get your respect and support; if they don't, they won't. Sticking to a guideline one day and letting it slide the next confuses children and ultimately teaches them that rules don't mean much. After a while they just stop paying attention, believing "it doesn't matter what I do because I can't control the outcome," which fosters a sense of helplessness and opens the door to depression.

Children also learn the rules—even when you don't spell them out—by watching and imitating you. For instance, children who hear their parents boasting about cheating on their tax returns may think that cheating on a book report or a test is acceptable, too. Children who know Mom or Dad "borrows" supplies from the workplace may interpret that to mean they can "borrow" items they want from school or the local department store. Teaching clear, predictable rules to children isn't just creating regulations; it's demonstrating these guidelines every day.

PRESENT A UNIFIED MESSAGE

It's important for parents not to give their children conflicting messages, particularly when it comes to child-rearing issues. Kids need consistency; if Mom insists that her child practice his piano lessons every day but Dad says he doesn't have to because music lessons aren't important, the child can feel confused. If you and your mate contradict each other all the time, your child can feel very insecure and become much more vulnerable to depression.

That doesn't mean you and your spouse always have to agree or that you must keep your differences from your children. It does mean, however, that you need to take time to work out your differences at least to the point where you can present a clear, consistent message to your kids.

Suppose, for instance, that your fifteen-year-old daughter wants to go to a concert that won't be over until 2:00 A.M. When she asks Dad, he flatly refuses. Mom, on the other hand, isn't so sure. You can say to your child, "Dad and I disagree, so you're going to have to wait until we discuss it before we give you an answer." Then try your best to work it out. You might explain to your husband that since your child is very responsible and has never broken a curfew, you feel she should be allowed to go. If he agrees in principle but is worried about how she'll get home, let your daughter know that and say something like, "You can go to the concert, but we need to arrange to have an adult we know pick you up and take you home." Or ask *her* to come up with a plan that will make everyone comfortable.

Another point: If you have very young kids, strive for continuity between you and your children's other caregivers. If you have a child in day care, for example, you want to make an effort to work with her teachers to coordinate home and day-care rules and routines. Your youngster will feel more secure knowing that she is expected to take a nap after lunch at home and at school.

Of course, total consistency isn't always possible or practical. But you can explain any inconsistencies to your child clearly and carefully. For instance, if you allow shouting in your home but the day-care teacher insists that children keep their voices down, you can explain, "There are two voices you can use. Your big voice is for playing at home or outside, and your little voice is for day care." That way, you provide predictability while promoting adaptability.

- **Principle #3: Fostering Open and Honest Communication**
  Your children need to know that they can talk to you openly and honestly about anything, to understand that you are always ready to answer their questions, share their joys and accomplishments, help them work through their frustrations, and understand their fears. Knowing that they can turn to you for help from the time they're very young—when the most important thing on their minds may be fig- uring out how to deal with the bully on the school bus—makes it more likely that they'll come to you when their problems are more complex and risky, like learning how to handle peer pressure regarding sex, drugs, or alcohol.

Good communication between you and your kids also prevents them from feeling that they have to keep troubling emotions bottled up inside, a situation that can make children feel overwhelmed and vulnerable to depression. When your kids know that they can talk about their problems and feelings, they have a great coping tool at their disposal: they can come to you for guidance and support when they run into a problem that they simply don't know how to handle. Children who don't have this tool—who believe that they're alone in facing life's challenges—are much more vulnerable to sadness, self-defeat, and isolation, all of which undermine their resiliency and put them at risk for depression.

BE SENSITIVE TO YOUR CHILDREN'S FEELINGS AND PERCEPTIONS

Giving your youngsters a quick, curt response or, worse, a reprimand whenever they bring up something that's troubling them will discourage any further discussion. Instead, respond in a way that tells your kids you're always willing to lend an understanding and empathetic ear.

For instance, if your youngster says, "I'm worried about the spelling test tomorrow," don't respond with "That's silly. You can't start worrying every time you have a test." Instead, say something like "I used to get nervous before tests, too. Most people do. So let's sit down and go over the words together."

STICK TO THE TRUTH

Children need to know that they can count on you for truthful, accurate information about any subject. If you repeatedly lie to your kids, you will never gain their trust. So tell the truth even when the news is bad.

For example, suppose the family's aging cat becomes very ill and your six-year-old comes to you and says, "I'm scared. Will Spunky die?" Try not to falsely reassure your youngster. Instead, say something like "I'm a little worried, too, because Spunky is very sick. And sometimes when cats are as old as Spunky they do die. But the vet is taking good care of him, and there's a good chance he'll be able to come home again." This simple, straightforward response lets your child know that she can always trust your words and that you think she is strong enough to handle the truth. In time, this trust will help her feel secure and safe not only with you but also with the world around her.

- **Principle #4: Adopting a Constructive, Balanced Approach to Discipline**

For too long, we've thought of discipline only as a means of punishing a child for actions we don't like or condone. But if we reframe this negative notion of discipline and start thinking about it from a more positive perspective—understanding that we shape our children's behavior not only by saying no when they do something wrong but also by saying yes when they do something right—then we can do a great deal to make our children more resilient and, therefore, more resistant to depression.

Parents need to find a balance between doling out punishment and offering encouragement and positive reinforcement. That is, if we place too much emphasis on punishment and barrage our kids with negative attention, they begin to feel as if there's something wrong with them, as if nothing they do is right. On the other hand, if we never say no to our kids, they grow up with an unrealistic view of themselves. Once they get out into the real world and face situations in which their actions are not always praised and valued, they can have great difficulty coping, which can place them at high risk for depression.

Here follow two important tactics to help achieve a more constructive, balanced approach to discipline.

SEPARATE THE BEHAVIOR FROM THE CHILD

Suppose your child repeatedly does something that makes you upset, like losing her belongings. If you criticize her, saying "Why are you so careless? We can't keep replacing everything you lose," you are sending the message that she (not just her action) is bad. She can begin to develop a negative self-image, become overly self-critical and more easily depressed.

If, however, you focus on the act—not the person—by saying "I get very frustrated when you lose your things. I don't think you do it on purpose, and I don't love you any less, but we need to work on this problem together so we can find a solution," you're conveying a very different message. Now you're letting her know that she is a good, lovable person, but that this particular behavior needs to be changed and that you're prepared to help.

SET UP APPROPRIATE CONSEQUENCES AND ALLOW FOR REPARATIONS

No normal, healthy child behaves perfectly all the time. When your eight-year-old accidentally breaks a neighbor's window during a forbidden game of hardball, she needs to know that there will be consequences for her action. And the best consequences are those that not only fit the child's age but relate to the problem. That is, instead of just grounding your youngster for a day or two, have her apologize to the neighbor and ask what she can do to make amends—perhaps helping to pick up and install the new window or assisting with other household chores. At any age letting a child know that there are consequences for her actions and, in most cases, a way to remedy the mistake not only helps to discourage the bad behavior, but also empowers the youngster and helps her feel better about herself.

Once your child has dealt with the consequences and made reparations, put the incident in the past. That way, your child learns that he can make a mistake, accept the consequences, learn from the experience, and move on to make a fresh start, without having previous events held against him.

■ Principle #5: Allowing Children to Experience Life

Most parents love their children so deeply that they want to shield them from life's pain, to put their youngsters in a protective bubble that will keep them forever happy and safe. This natural warmth and protectiveness is further fostered by our society which places enormous pressure on parents to create a perfect, idyllic world for their kids.

But life *isn't* perfect or idyllic, even for children. Every day, kids encounter frustrations and disappointments that even the most astute and loving parents cannot foresee or prevent. And perhaps that's how it should be. Because only through experiencing and successfully coping with the stresses, challenges, and frustrations of everyday life can children learn to face their problems and still bounce back. Although well intentioned, parents who try too hard to protect their children from life's difficulties risk raising emotionally fragile youngsters who are extremely vulnerable to depression as well as other emotional problems.

I recently worked with a bright fifteen-year-old whose story poignantly illustrates this idea. Charlotte had become clinically depressed following a breakup with her first serious boyfriend. "For as long as I can remember," she told me during one of our early sessions, "I wanted to have a dog. But no matter how many times I asked, my parents refused. The reason, they said, was that they didn't want me to feel bad when the dog died. As I grew up, they tried to protect me from everything bad. They never told me about family illnesses, for example. I was away at camp when my grandmother died last year, and they didn't even tell me about that. I didn't find out until I came home."

As we worked together, it became clear that this teenager had not had enough opportunity early on to learn how to cope with the stressful aspects of life, to build up her emotional fortitude gradually by dealing first with the routine problems of early childhood and then with the more diverse and complex dilemmas of the school-age and adolescent years. As a result, she had come to believe that she was incapable of coping with such problems, which damaged her self-esteem and made her more vulnerable to depression following the breakup of her first romantic relationship.

Allowing children to experience frustrations, upsets, and disappointments gives them important practice in coping with life's many challenges. Now I'm not suggesting that you intentionally introduce stress into your children's lives, allow them to become *devastated* by disappointment, or deliberately set them up to fail. But I am recommending that you try not to shield your kids from life's various ups and downs. Think about it this way: Allowing kids to experience life's good and bad moments provides a kind of emotional inoculation that helps children build a healthy, natural resistance to emotional difficulties like depression.

LET KIDS BE KIDS

Just like adults, children need to strike a healthy balance in their lives. While participating in organized sports and other activities—art classes, music lessons, enrichment programs—is important, so is exploring the world in a spontaneous, unstructured way. Children certainly profit from well-designed, age-appropriate programmed activities, but they also benefit from free time in which they can play, let off steam, daydream, reflect, and simply be kids. If children are over-programmed, they can become so stressed that they are more vulnerable to depression.

NURTURE MULTIPLE TALENTS AND INTERESTS

Most children have many areas of interest and a natural curiosity to explore them. You want to encourage such exploration, without forcing them to specialize too early. If you focus exclusively on one of your child's interests or talents too soon, you can rob her of the chance to develop an array of interests and to learn from diverse opportunities, experiences, and interactions.

Suppose, for instance, your child has a gift for dancing. Giving her ballet lessons and encouraging this talent is wonderful—and very important. And insisting that she study ballet to the exclusion of everything else—demanding that she take so many dance classes that she never has time to play with the other kids on the block and build important social skills—may make her an outstanding dancer. But it won't help her develop the range of emotional tools she needs to become a strong, resilient individual.

■ Principle #6: Enhancing Self-Esteem

Over the years that I've practiced child psychiatry, I have come to believe this important idea: *Children with a healthy sense of self-esteem are the most resilient and best able to resist depression.* There are several ways to help your child develop a positive self-image. Here follow some of the most essential.

NURTURE AN "I-CAN-DO-IT" ATTITUDE

Children who develop depression often feel that they are powerless to shape the situations in which they find themselves. If they don't get to stay up late and watch a special TV program, it's because Mommy and Daddy are "mean," not because they didn't pick up their toys as they'd promised. If they fail a test, it's because they're "stupid," not because they didn't study enough. But kids who are raised to believe that they are active participants in the world, that what they do affects how things turn out, don't feel this sense of helplessness and, therefore, are much more resistant to depression. When a problem arises, they believe they have the ability and resources to find a solution.

One of the simplest ways to foster this I-can-do-it attitude even in very young children is to give them a choice in their everyday affairs. A toddler can decide whether he wants an apple or yogurt for a snack; a preschooler can choose whether to wear his red or blue sweatshirt to play outside. A school-age child can pick the color paint for his room in the new house, and a teenager can decide whether he wants to go out for basketball or join the school newspaper.

On the other hand, you don't want to give children a choice in things about which they really have no say. That can only damage the sense of trust and honesty you have established. So if your job demands that you and your family relocate, don't ask your child if he wants to move. Let him know you're anxious to hear his feelings about the change, but don't let him believe that he has a choice in the matter if he really doesn't.

Nurturing a sense of self-confidence goes hand in hand with encouraging children to play to their strengths. We've already discussed the importance of self-awareness in this process. Encouraging kids to be sensitive to their own unique traits and personality styles can help them create positive, affirming life experiences for themselves. But take this one step further and we see that developing an I-can-do-it attitude depends not only on encouraging self-awareness in your children, but also on helping them use that self-awareness to develop strategies to achieve their goals no matter how out of reach they may at first seem.

Suppose your animal-loving child wants to become a veterinarian and is extremely upset because he's gotten a D in his first biology class. Instead of discouraging him from trying to realize his dream, sit down with your child and together try to come up with some realistic ways to reach his goal, such as getting a tutor, or enrolling in summer school. In this way you help your child learn to assess himself accurately and use that assessment to develop a can-do attitude that acknowledges his weaknesses but accentuates his strengths.

CELEBRATE YOUR CHILDREN'S SUCCESSES

Since kids come with a desire to learn and a natural curiosity built in, I believe that opportunities to test out their skills and discover their strengths arise constantly in children's everyday lives. All you have to do is recognize, encourage, and reinforce them.

For instance, when your preschooler plays on a swing and boasts "Look how high I can go," taking great pride in her accomplishment, you want to share your child's excitement and enthusiasm by saying something like "I see. You're getting to be such a big girl that you can pump all by yourself!" If your six-year-old builds a tower, carefully placing one block on top of another until they all balance, share his sense of achievement and joy by saying "What a great tower! You're such a good builder!"

Try the same approach with older children; just adjust materials or activities to fit their age. For instance, teaching your school-age son to swim by gradually introducing him to the water, and giving your unqualified praise (and positive reinforcement) as he learns to dog-paddle, float, and eventually, swim the length of the pool, provides a perfect series of opportunities to help nurture his sense of mastery and reinforce his self-esteem.

DON'T MAKE YOUR APPROVAL CONTINGENT ON YOUR CHILD'S SUCCESS

We all want our children to succeed, and we praise them when they do—when they get a gold star for the picture they drew, or an A on a history test, when they make the honor roll or the basketball team. All that's fine—unless the *only* time we praise them is when they bring home the trophy (either literally or figuratively).

Children who grow up believing that their parents love them only when they achieve or succeed are exceptionally vulnerable to an exaggerated sense of disappointment, poor self-esteem, overwhelming sadness, and, ultimately, depression, when they fail. And everyone fails now and again—it's part of life and the learning process.

So be sure to let your child know that your love is unconditional. Don't assume she understands; instead, demonstrate it again and again. Even a small comment like "I'm really proud of you for going out for band. I want you to know that whether or not you make it, you're a great kid and I love you very much" can go a long way in helping your child know she's loved and appreciated for who she is, not just for what she does.

This also means not being overly critical. If your child proudly brings you the picture he drew in his first coloring book, don't point out that he didn't stay in the lines. Instead, emphasize the positive by saying something like "What a great picture. I love the bright colors you chose." Then hang the artwork on the refrigerator door so that your child knows you truly value what he does.

Similarly, should your teenager bring home a report card with six A's and one B in history, try not to respond with "What happened in history?" even if you say it as a joke. Instead, offer something like "I'm really proud of you. All that hard work you did this semester really paid off."

Giving your child approval whether or not he meets your standards of success also requires a measure of self-awareness on your part. You don't want to become a "stage parent," trying to fulfill your unmet goals and aspirations through your child. Instead, you want to recognize that your child is a separate individual with his own dreams and priorities. He needs to be supported, not pushed.

MODEL GOOD COPING BEHAVIORS

Children also learn by example. You teach them through your actions, not just your words. Thus, you can help your child develop positive self-esteem and good coping skills by practicing them yourself and letting your youngster follow your lead.

Here's an example: Suppose you're driving your child to Little League practice one Saturday morning—and running a little late—when your car unexpectedly runs out of gas. What do you do? Do you get upset, throw your hands up in the air, and bemoan your bad luck? Or do you stay calm, figure out a way to get to the nearest gas station, and take care of the problem?

If you take the former tack, you're teaching your child that frustrations and setbacks can overwhelm and defeat. If you take the latter approach, you demonstrate that you have the power and skill to find a way around life's obstacles without becoming overwhelmed.

Another example: You're passed over for the promotion you wanted and you feel upset, disappointed, probably even angry. Your child might notice that you're not yourself and ask you what's wrong. It's important not only to let him know what's bothering you—"I thought I was going to get a new job at work, but I didn't"—but also to show him that a disappointment isn't the end of the world, and that you are going to start looking for another job or figuring out a better way to get the kind of position you want. Seeing you send out résumés and phoning your contacts lets him know that people can take action to overcome life's setbacks.

INTERPRET EXPERIENCES POSITIVELY

Even when your child does fail, you can always find a way to interpret the experience positively. Do this often and consistently enough and you'll help him do the same. Suppose, for example, your two-year-old falls down at the playground, gets up, looks down at his scratched palm, and immediately starts to cry. If you respond by giving him a hug and saying, "Oh, you got hurt. My poor little boy," you underscore his sad, helpless feelings. But if you add "You're so big and strong. Even though you got a little scratch, you got right up again," you convey a much more positive, affirming message.

Suppose your nine-year-old soccer player lets three goals get past him during an important play-off game, and as you're driving home together later, he says, "I hate soccer. I stink at it and I'm never playing again!" Saying "I know it's hard to lose, but I'm really proud of you for hanging in there and doing your best. You're really a tough, brave kid" puts the situation in a much brighter light.

Eventually, your child borrows such positive, affirming approaches from you, tries them on, and makes them his own. In this process, he begins to build his resiliency and strengthen his ability to cope with negative experiences without feeling overwhelmed and, eventually, depressed.

Because You Can't Do It All

Mothers, fathers, and other important caregivers who follow the six principles of parenting for resiliency can go a long way toward preventing depression in their children. But don't blame yourself if, despite your good efforts, your child does become depressed. Some children, whether because of biological factors, traumatic experiences, or a combination of both, develop depression even when their moms and dads are the best possible parents. But keep in mind that even if depression occurs, using the techniques of parenting for resiliency—combined with early recognition and treatment—will speed your child's recovery and help reduce the likelihood (or, at the very least, the intensity) of future depressive episodes.

It's also important to remember that no parent can do it all, all the time. There will be instances when you might not be able to offer your children the most stable environment, perhaps because your community is being rezoned and your child must switch schools. Or maybe you can't protect your child from suffering a blow to his self-esteem when he gets rejected by the school of his choice.

But even when a particular situation keeps you from applying one of the six tenets of parenting for resiliency, you can still help prevent your child's depression. How? By putting more emphasis on the remaining principles.

Let's say that your company relocates and your family has to move across the country, a situation that can't help but undermine the predictability and stability of your child's world, at least for a period of time. That's when you need to work even harder at other principles, like keeping lines of communication open and enhancing his self-esteem. So when you're spending some time alone with your youngster, try talking with him about the move and encouraging him to express his feelings. As for encouraging self-esteem, emphasize his talents. If your child is musical, you might encourage him to join the band at his new school, or audition for the community center choir. And you might make an extra effort to find a good music teacher in your new neighborhood, to show up for recitals, and to enthusiastically express your pride in his accomplishments. Encouraging him to talk about his feelings and to focus on his strengths are great ways to help offset some of the problems generated by the temporary loss of stability in his life.

Remember the simple rule of thumb: Pay attention to what you *can* do to compensate for what you cannot. If you keep this in mind, you'll be able to parent for resiliency, no matter what the circumstances.

A Closing Word

Depression is a serious illness that each year affects all too many children and teenagers. But it is also an identifiable and treatable problem—and, in many cases, a preventable one. By using the principles and techniques we've discussed in this chapter, you can help your children learn to cope with any situation that life presents them with and greatly reduce their risk of developing clinical depression. In short, parenting for resiliency will help you raise happier, more adaptable, self-confident children who will grow into self-assured, emotionally healthy adults.

Afterword

We have come a long way in identifying and treating clinical depression in children. We even know something about how we can prevent this illness, or at least reduce children's risk. Still, we don't have all the answers. And we have a long way to go until we can make depression an illness of the past.

Yet, as I said at the outset of this book, I am hopeful. When I look at some of the research being done—work centering on neurobiology, genetics, and new approaches to treatment—I see a future in which we will be able to reduce the suffering that depression brings.

But until then, there is much parents and others concerned about the health and well-being of today's youth can do in a preventive way to decrease the likelihood and even incidence of depression in children. In the final chapter of this book, I've suggested specific parenting techniques that will help you do just that. Additionally, however, I believe we need to advocate for increased funding for mental health research, particularly for children. In this time of change and transition for America's health care system, we also need to push for much greater emphasis on preventive mental health care for children and adults. What's more, we need to encourage our schools to play a more significant role in identifying students with emotional difficulties and assisting them in getting the help they need.

Finally, we need to do whatever we can to educate Americans about depression and eliminate the stigma that still surrounds this all-too-common condition. That is already beginning to occur. I see more and more individuals—some of whom are quite well known, such as Mike Wallace, Judy Collins, and William Styron—willing to speak out about their personal experiences with depression. I applaud them for their courage and support them for their efforts to spread this most important message: that today almost no child or adult need suffer from depression. If detected early and diagnosed accurately, depression can be effectively treated—and, finally, overcome.

Helpful Organizations and Resources

General Mental Health Information and Help with Referrals

American Academy of Child and Adolescent Psychiatry
3615 Wisconsin Avenue, N.W.
Washington, DC 20016
(202) 966-7300
1-800-333-7636
World Wide Web address: http://www.aacap.org

American Academy of Pediatrics
141 Northwest Point Boulevard
P.O. Box 927
Elk Grove Village, IL 60009-0927
(847) 228-5005
1-800-433-9016
E-mail: kidsdocs@aap.org.
World Wide Web address: http://www.aap.org

American Association of Marriage and Family Therapy
1133 15th Street, N.W.
Suite 300
Washington, DC 20005
(202) 452-0109
E-mail: aamft.org
Send SASE for listing of therapists in your area.

American Psychiatric Association
Division of Public Affairs
1400 K Street, N.W.
Washington, DC 20005
(202) 682-6142
E-mail: m.bennet@apa.org
World Wide Web address: http://www.psych.org

American Psychological Association
750 First Street, N.E.
Washington, DC 20002-4242
(202) 336-5700
World Wide Web address: http://www.apa.org

Association for the Care of Children's Health
7910 Woodmont Avenue
Suite 300
Bethesda, MD 20814
(301) 654-6549
1-800-808-2224
E-mail: acch@clark.net
World Wide Web address: http://www.wsd.com/acch.org

Center for Mental Health Services' Knowledge Exchange
   Network
P.O. Box 42490
Washington, DC 20015
1-800-789-2647
Electronic bulletin board (dial from computer): 1-800-790-2647

Children's Rights of America
8735 Dunwoody Place
Suite 6
Atlanta, GA 30350
(770) 998-6698
Operates the National Youth Crisis Hotline—1-800-442-4673 (a
twenty-four-hour emergency number for kids who are suicidal,
being abused, etc.)

Federation of Families for Children's Mental Health
1021 Prince Street
Alexandria, VA 22314
(703) 684-7710
E-mail: ffcmh@crosslink.com

Maternal and Child Health Bureau
Health Resources and Services Administration
Public Health Services
5600 Fishers Lane
Rockville, MD 20857
(301) 443-0205
World Wide Web address: http://www.os.dhhs.gov/hrsa/mchb

National Association of Social Workers
750 First Street, N.E.
Suite 700
Washington, DC 20002-4242
(202) 408-8600
1-800-638-8799
E-mail: nasw@capcon.net

National Maternal and Child Health Clearinghouse
2070 Chain Bridge Road
Suite 450
Vienna, VA 22182-2536
(703) 821-8955

Organizations That Credential Therapists

American Association of State Social Work Boards
400 South Ridge Parkway
Suite B
Culpeper, VA 22701
1-800-225-6880

American Board of Professional Psychology
2100 East Broadway
Suite 313
Columbia, MO 65201
(573) 875-1267

American Board of Psychiatry and Neurology
500 Lake Cook Road
Deerfield, IL 60015
(847) 945-7900

Federation of State Medical Boards
Federation Place
400 Fuller Wiser Road
Suite 300
Euless, TX 76039
(817) 868-4000
World Wide Web address: http://www.fsmb.org
(Does not credential psychiatrists itself, but will refer you to appropriate state medical board. Web page also lists state medical boards.)

Information and Referral on Clinical Depression

Center for Mental Health Services
Knowledge Exchange Network
P.O. Box 42490
Washington, DC 20015
1-800-789-2647
World Wide Web address: http://www.mentalhealth.org/
E-mail: ken@mentalhealth.org

Depression and Related Affective Disorders Association
    (DRADA)
Johns Hopkins University School of Medicine
Meyer 3-181
600 North Wolfe Street
Baltimore, MD 21287
(410) 955-4647
(202) 955-5800 (Washington, D.C., residents only)
E-mail: drada@welchlink.welch.jhu.edu

The Journey of Hope
c/o Louisiana Alliance for the Mentally Ill (L'AMI)
P.O. Box 2547
Baton Rouge, LA 70821
(504) 343-6928

National Alliance for the Mentally Ill
200 N. Glebe Road
Suite 1015
Arlington, VA 22203-3754
(703) 524-7600
1-800-950-6264
E-mail: namiofc@aol.com
World Wide Web address: http://www.cais.com/vikings/nami

Note: You can also contact NAMI's state and local affiliates, which use the name Alliance for the Mentally Ill, or AMI. (For example: AMI of Vermont, or AMI of Colorado.) Simply check the telephone directory for the location nearest you.

National Alliance for Research on Schizophrenia and Depression
60 Cutter Mill Road
Suite 404
Great Neck, NY 11021
(516) 829-0091
1-800-829-8289
World Wide Web address: http://www.mhsource.com

National Depressive and Manic Depressive Association
    (NDMDA)
730 North Franklin
Suite 501
Chicago, IL 60610
(312) 652-0049
1-800-826-3632 (1-800-82-NDMDA)

National Foundation for Depressive Illness
P.O. Box 2257
New York, NY 10016-2257
1-800-248-4344 (for recorded announcement)

National Institute of Mental Health (NIMH)
Depression Awareness, Recognition, and Treatment Program
    (DART)
National Institute of Mental Health
Dept. GL, Room 10-85
5600 Fishers Lane
Rockville, MD 20857
(301) 443-4140
1-800-421-4211

National Mental Health Association (NMHA)
National Public Education Campaign on Clinical Depression
1021 Prince Street
Alexandria, VA 22314-2971
(703) 684-7722
1-800-969-6642
World Wide Web address:
    http://www.worldcorp.com/dc-online/nhma/index.html

Note: *National Depression Screening Day*
Since 1991, NMHA has been one of the sponsors of National
Depression Screening Day, an annual one-day event (usually
held in October) offering adults and children free screenings for

depression at thousands of locations throughout the U.S. All screenings are conducted by licensed mental health professionals, and individual results are confidential. Participants are given further referrals following the screening when appropriate. For more information, call 1-800-969-NMHA.

Specialized Resources

Attention Deficit Disorder
>   Children and Adults with Attention Deficit Disorder (CH.A.D.D.)
>   499 Northwest 70th Avenue
>   Suite 101
>   Plantation, FL 33317
>   (954) 587-3700
>   1-800-233-4050
>   E-mail: "majordomo@mv.mv.com"

Child Abuse
>   National Committee to Prevent Child Abuse (NCPCA)
>   P.O. Box 2866
>   Chicago, IL 60690
>   (312) 663-3520
>   1-800-55-NCPCA
>   World Wide Web address: http://www.childabuse.org

Eating Disorders
>   National Association of Anorexia Nervosa and Associated
>   Disorders
>   P.O. Box 7
>   Highland Park, IL 60035
>   (847) 831-3438

Homosexuality
>   The Hetrick-Martin Institute
>   2 Astor Place
>   New York, NY 10003-6998
>   (212) 674-2400

PFLAG
(Parents, Families and Friends of Lesbians and Gays)
1101 14th Street, N.W.
Suite 1030
Washington, DC 20005
(202) 638-4200
E-mail: pflag@aol.com

Suicide

American Association of Suicidology
4201 Connecticut Avenue, N.W.
Suite 310
Washington, DC 20008
(202) 237-2280
E-mail: mcdO117W@wonder.em.cdc.gov

The American Suicide Foundation
1045 Park Avenue
New York, NY 10028
1-800-273-4042
E-mail: 76433,1676@compuserve.com

Learning Disabilities

Learning Disabilities Association of America
4156 Library Road
Pittsburgh, PA 15234
(412) 341-8077
World Wide Web address: httpp:///www.vcu.edu/eduweb/

National Center for Learning Disabilities
381 Park Avenue South
Suite 1420
New York, NY 10016
(212) 545-7510

Obsessive-Compulsive Disorder

The Obsessive-Compulsive Foundation
P.O. Box 70
Milford, CT 06460-0070
(203) 878-5669
E-mail: jph28a@prodigy.com
World Wide Web address:
    http://pages.prodigy.com/a/willen/ofc.html

Substance Abuse
    Al-Anon Family Groups
    P.O. Box 862
    Midtown Station
    New York, NY 10018-0862
    1-800-356-9996

    National Clearinghouse for Alcohol and Drug Information
      (NCADI)
    11426 Rockville Pike
    Rockville, MD 20852
      or
    P.O. Box 2345
    Rockville, MD 20847-2345
    1-800-729-6686
    E-mail: info@prevline.health.org
    World Wide Web address: http://www.health.org

    National Council on Alcoholism and Drug Dependence (NCADD)
    12 West 21st Street, 7th Floor
    New York, NY 10010
    1-800-622-2255

    National Families in Action
    2296 Henderson Mill Road
    Suite 300
    Atlanta, GA 30345
    (770) 934-6364
    World Wide Web address: http://wwww.emory.edu/nfia

Additional Reading

For Parents

Chess, Stella, and Alexander Thomas. *Know Your Child: An Authoritative Guide for Today's Parents.* New York: Basic Books, 1987.

Dumas, Lynne S. *Talking with Your Child About a Troubled World.* New York: Fawcett Columbine, 1992.

Fishman, Katharine Davis. *Behind the One-Way Mirror: Psychotherapy and Children.* New York: Bantam, 1995.

Hallowell, Edward M. *When You Worry About the Child You Love.* New York: Simon & Schuster, 1996.

Hallowell, Edward M., and John Ratey. *Driven to Distraction.* New York: Pantheon, 1994.

Ingersoll, Barbara D., and Sam Goldstein. *Lonely, Sad and Angry.* New York: Doubleday, 1995.

Kerns, Lawrence L., with Adrienne B. Lieberman. *Helping Your Depressed Child.* Rocklin, Calif.: Prima Publishing, 1993.

Koplewicz, Harold. *It's Nobody's Fault: New Hope and Help for Difficult Children and Their Parents.* New York: Random House, 1996.

Kroen, William C. *Helping Children Cope with the Loss of a Loved One.* Minneapolis: Free Spirit Publishing, 1996.

Papolos, Demitri, and Janice Papolos. *Overcoming Depression.* Rev. ed. New York: HarperCollins, 1992.

Seligman, Martin E. P., with Karen Reivich, Lisa Jaycox, and Jane Gillham. *The Optimistic Child*. New York: Houghton Mifflin, 1995.

Turecki, Stanley, with Sarah Wernick. *Normal Children Have Problems, Too*. New York: Bantam, 1994.

For Children

Hamilton, DeWitt, illustrated by Gail Owens. *Sad Days, Glad Days: A Story About Depression*. Morton Grove, Ill.: Albert Whitman & Company, 1995. (Parents should read the book with their children ages four through seven; also appropriate for children ages eight through eleven.)

Hipp, Earl. *Fighting Invisible Tigers: A Stress Management Guide for Teens*. Rev. ed. Minneapolis: Free Spirit Publishing, 1995.

Hyde, Margaret O., and Elizabeth H. Forsyth. *Know About Mental Illness*. New York: Walker and Company, 1996. (Ages 8–12)

Kaufman, Gershen, and Lev Raphael. *Stick Up for Yourself! Every Kid's Guide to Personal Power and Positive Self-Esteem*. Minneapolis: Free Spirit Publishing, 1990. (Ages 8–12)

Nelson, Richard E., and Judith Galas. *The Power to Prevent Suicide: A Guide for Teens Helping Teens*. Minneapolis: Free Spirit Publishing, 1994. (Ages 8–12)

Payne, Lauren Murphy, illustrated by Claudia Rohling. *Just Because I Am: A Child's Book of Affirmation*. Minneapolis: Free Spirit Publishing, 1994. (Ages 3–8)

Simon, Norma, illustrated by Joe Lasker. *How Do I Feel?* Morton Grove, Ill.: Albert Whitman & Company, 1970. (Ages 4–7)

About the Authors

David G. Fassler

David G. Fassler, M.D., is a practicing child and adolescent psychiatrist who specializes in the prevention of psychiatric disorders in children and adolescents. He serves as the director of Child and Adolescent Psychiatry for Choate Health Systems and Choate Health Management in Stoneham, Massachusetts, and as clinical director of Otter Creek Associates in Burlington, Vermont. Through these positions, he has overseen the development of a comprehensive system of clinical programs for children, adolescents, and their families.

Dr. Fassler is also clinical associate professor in the Department of Psychiatry at the University of Vermont. He is the founder and clinical psychiatric consultant of the PlayCare Center preschool programs in Richmond and Burlington, Vermont.

Dr. Fassler is a member of the Work Group on Consumer Issues of the American Academy of Child and Adolescent Psychiatry and chair of the Committee on Psychiatry and Mental Health in the Schools of the American Psychiatric Association. He also coordinates National Depression Screening Day activities on behalf of the Academy, and has served as the principal investigator on a National Institute of Mental Health training grant focusing on the diagnosis, assessment, and treatment of depression.

Dr. Fassler is the editor of *Emergency Medical Intervention with the Alcoholic Patient*, published by Gardner Press, and the coauthor of a series of children's books including *What's a Virus, Anyway? The Kids' Book About AIDS, The Divorce Workbook: A Guide for Kids and Families, Changing Families: A Guide for Kids and Grown-Ups*, and *Coming to America: The Kids' Book About Immigration*, all published by Waterfront Books.

Dr. Fassler is a graduate of the Yale University School of Medicine. He completed his training in adult psychiatry at the University of Vermont, and in child psychiatry at Cambridge Hospital, Harvard Medical School. He lives and practices in Burlington, Vermont.

Lynne S. Dumas

Lynne S. Dumas is a former teacher turned freelance writer who has written extensively on the psychological aspects of children's and families' lives. She is the author of *Talking with Your Child About a Troubled World* (Fawcett Columbine, 1992) and the coauthor of *Congratulations! You've Been Fired: Sound Advice for Women Who've Been Terminated, Laid Off, Pink-Slipped, Downsized or Otherwise Unemployed* (Fawcett Colum-bine, 1990) and *Midlife Can Wait: How to Stay Young and Healthy After Age 35* (Ballantine, 1995). Her many magazine articles have appeared in such national publications as *Working Mother*, *Woman's Day*, *Cosmopolitan*, *Family Circle*, *New Woman*, *McCall's*, *Sesame Street Parent's Guide*, *Psychology Today*, and *Health*. She is also the managing editor of *America's Agenda*, Scholastic, Inc.'s educational newsmagazine.

Lynne Dumas holds a B.A. cum laude from Barnard College and an M.A. from Columbia University. She is a member of the American Society of Journalists and Authors and lives with her family in New York City.

Index